ASPECTS OF BIRMINGHAM

ASPECTS *of* BIRMINGHAM

Discovering Local History

Edited by

Brian Hall

Series Editor
Brian Elliott

Wharncliffe Books

This book is dedicated to Dorothy McCulla
who inspired so many of us.

First Published in 2001 by
Wharncliffe Books
an imprint of
Pen and Sword Books Limited,
47 Church Street, Barnsley,
South Yorkshire. S70 2AS

Copyright © Wharncliffe Books 2001

For up-to-date information on other titles produced under the
Wharncliffe imprint, please telephone or write to:

> **Wharncliffe Books**
> **FREEPOST**
> **47 Church Street**
> **Barnsley**
> **South Yorkshire S70 2BR**
> **Telephone (24 hours): 01226 - 734555**

ISBN: 1-871647-67-3

A CIP catalogue record of this book is available from the
British Library

Cover illustration: *New Street, Birmingham.*

Printed in the United Kingdom by
CPI UK

CONTENTS

INTRODUCTION
by Brian Hall

Anyone interested in local history cannot fail to have noticed the enormous upsurge in interest in the subject over the last thirty years or so. The numbers accessing local history collections and archives in libraries and record offices continue to grow.

There are many reasons for this. There has always been an inherent interest in local history by people from all social and educational background but the pace of change in society is now so fast that people cannot help but be aware of the past disappearing, literally, before their eyes. Many have resolved do play their part in helping to preserve something of **their** past. The number of local history societies continues to grow, not just in their traditional middle-class suburbs but in working-class communities as well. Local history is not just nostalgia but can be a very real social, educational and political force within a community. In addition, many academics, at all levels, have found local history rich in opportunities for research, partly because many national topics and collections have been over-researched, and partly because much more intimate studies are possible if conducted at a local level. In schools too, often under the subject of 'environmental studies' children have found local history to be a fascinating and rewarding area for study. This change really only came about from the 1960s – before that 'history' nearly always meant national, international or ancient history.

There are, therefore, large numbers of people of all ages engaged in some aspect of local history research and many of them are amateurs or children. The contributions of these groups should never be underestimated. They bring to local history a freshness of approach and a genuine empathy with the area. Most English local history is still to be written and amateur historians will write most of it.

The history of Birmingham, once renowned as 'the workshop of the empire' is brought together in eleven pinpoint studies of the city's life and leisure. **Birmingham Municipal Bank**, the only such enterprise successfully operated by a city council, here rubs shoulders with some **Lesser-known 'characters'** of the city. The work of both the **Birmingham Mission** and the **Birmingham Children's Emigration Homes** is examined. In keeping with its great civic pride, during the troubled times of the 1930s, Birmingham held a **great Pageant** and while war clouds gathered over Europe, the young men of Birmingham took part in the **Spanish Civil War**. Two other great achievements of the city are explored in **Hazelwood School**, once compared favourably with Rugby School, and the work of **Waller Jeffs**, a pioneer of film-making. One of the sadder aspects of the city's history is reflected in the study of **Workhouses**. There is also a fascinating study of female representation on the city council in **Fit and Proper Councillors?** and a portrayal of **Col. Fred Burnaby**, a prominent Birmingham Conservative and reputedly, at one time, the strongest man in the British army! All these contributions represent a very varied collection of aspects from Birmingham's wonderful and colourful history. There are already offers of contributions for a second volume and the editor would be delighted to hear from anyone interested in making a contribution for future volumes. If Barnsley is worth six volumes (at the last count), Birmingham is surely capable of much more!

1. BIRMINGHAM WORKHOUSE MASTERS AND MATRONS IN THE 1830S AND 1840S

by Paul Tolley

Introduction

THIS STUDY FOCUSES ATTENTION upon some of the masters (or governors) and matrons who were in charge of the Birmingham, Aston and Kings Norton Union Workhouses during the early years of the New Poor Law of 1834. The study has been developed from my PhD and MA research into the administration and politics of the Poor Law in the Parish of Birmingham and the Aston and Kings Norton Unions during the nineteenth and early twentieth centuries.[1]

As other writers have emphasised, workhouse masters and matrons played a key role in implementing Poor Law policy at the local level.[2] It was the central Poor Law agency, the Poor Law Commission (PLC) from 1834-47 and the Poor Law Board (PLB) from 1847-71, together with local boards of guardians, who determined and directed Poor Law policies and administration following the enactment of the *1834 Poor Law Amendment Act*. However, it was the officers, such as the workhouse master and matron, who were responsible for day to day operations.

Workhouse masters and matrons, though accountable to boards of guardians and the PLC/ PLB, exercised a very considerable degree of power and authority in the institutions over which they presided. Under such circumstances, it is perhaps unsurprising that some masters and matrons were tempted to abuse their position. This is not to say that the notorious example of the master of the Andover Workhouse was typical.[3] In this study, the intention is to provide a balanced impression of how local Workhouse masters and matrons fulfilled their roles and the sort of difficulties which arose.

Poor Law Administration in Birmingham

From 1831 to 1912, the Birmingham Board of Guardians operated a separate poor relief system in the civil Parish of Birmingham, under the terms of a local *Guardians Act of 1831*, which had superseded an earlier local Act of 1783. The 1831 local Act was not overridden by the *1834 Poor Law Amendment Act*, under the terms of which the other Poor Law authorities in the district were established. However,

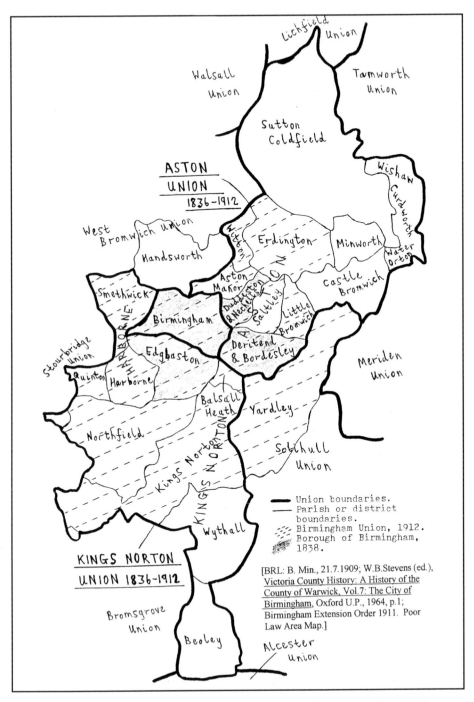

Union boundaries.
Parish or district boundaries.
Birmingham Union, 1912.
Borough of Birmingham, 1838.

[BRL: B. Min., 21.7.1909; W.B.Stevens (ed.), Victoria County History: A History of the County of Warwick, Vol.7: The City of Birmingham, Oxford U.P., 1964, p.1; Birmingham Extension Order 1911. Poor Law Area Map.]

Figure 1. Poor Law Authority Boundaries in the Birmingham Area 1836-1912. *Birmingham Reference Library.*

during the course of the nineteenth century the PLC and their successors did gradually assume greater influence over the affairs of the Birmingham Guardians. This situation parallels that in other places such as Coventry, Exeter and Southampton.[4]

The Aston Union, declared in October 1836, was responsible for the administration of poor relief in the Parishes of Aston, Curdworth, Sutton Coldfield and Wishaw, and the Hamlet of Minworth until 1912. Declared in November 1836, the Kings Norton Union was responsible for Poor Law administration in the Parishes of Beoley, Edgbaston, Harborne, Kings Norton and Northfield during the same period. Responsibility for Poor Law administration in the post-1838 Borough and later City of Birmingham was therefore split between the Birmingham, Aston and Kings Norton Boards of Guardians. In

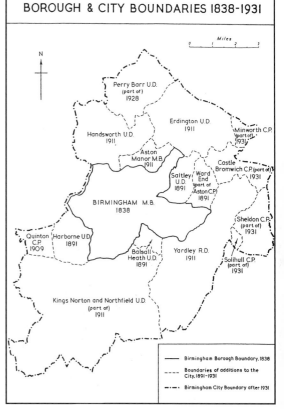

Figure 2. Birmingham Borough & City Boundaries 1838-1931. *Birmingham Reference Library.*

1912 the Aston and Kings Norton Unions ceased to exist when their constituent districts were transferred to the jurisdiction of a newly constituted Birmingham Union or other neighbouring Unions under the terms of the *1911 Greater Birmingham Act*.[5] (Figures 1 and 2)

Masters' and Matrons' Duties

Workhouse rules and regulations issued by the PLC to unions formed under the terms of the *1834 Poor Law Amendment Act* stipulated the duties of the various officers. The standard form of rules and regulations for union workhouses cited in the PLC's first annual report of 1835, lists the onerous duties and responsibilities of workhouse masters in 23 separate points and those of matrons in 10 separate points. In 1847 the PLC's General Consolidated Order, modified from time to time by later Orders, included sections regulating the appointment, terms of employment, duties and responsibilities of Poor Law officers.[6]

In 1844, as part of its campaign to assert its influence over such local Act Poor Law authorities as Birmingham, the PLC issued an Order detailing rules and regulations for the governance of the Birmingham Workhouse. This Order, and an 1850 PLB Order which superseded it, both included regulations relating to the appointment, qualifications, duties, remuneration, suspension and removal from office of Birmingham Board officers, including the Workhouse master and matron.[7] Prior to 1844, however, officers employed by the Birmingham Board were subject only to regulations issued by the Guardians under the terms of the local Act. Rules and regulations agreed by the Birmingham Guardians in 1818, revised in 1822 and 1841, included comprehensive sections relating to the Workhouse governor and matron.[8]

Advertisements for Birmingham Workhouse governors and matrons during the early 1840s, stated succinctly:

> *The Governor must be fully competent to keep the Books required by the Guardians, to superintend the Labour of the Paupers in the House, and otherwise to enforce the Regulations of the Guardians.*
>
> *The Matron will be required to understand the usual routine of Housekeeping and plain Cooking, and be able to superintend the Employment of the Females.*[9]

The Master and Matron of the Aston Union Workhouse, 1836-48
The Villages: Continuity, Salaries and Differences with the Schoolmistress

Thomas Village and his wife Ann served as master and matron of the Aston Union Workhouse at Erdington from the inception of the Aston Union until 1848, having previously served the Parish of Aston in the same capacity. Although they held continuous service, the Villages were not however appointed formally by the Board, and their appointments confirmed by the PLC, until October 1838.[10]

The Villages always retained the confidence of the Guardians, but questions relating to salary increases did prove divisive, a phenomenon not uncommon elsewhere. At the time of their formal appointment, it was decided that Mr and Mrs Village's salaries would remain at £42 and £21 per annum respectively, with board and 'the use of such provisions as the House afford.' Together with the schoolmistress and porter, they were also allowed an extra allowance of 2oz of tea, 10oz of butter and 14oz of sugar per week. In December 1838, the parsimonious Guardians did agree to increase the master's salary to £50 per annum and the matron's to £25 per annum, at which rates they remained until December 1841, when the Board increased their joint salary to £85 a year. Some Guardians, led by the Reverend W R Bedford, a vehement opponent of the New Poor Law, had initially succeeded in preventing an increase, but following further consideration the Board voted in favour. Subsequently PLC approval was given, although Assistant Commissioner Robert Weale expressed his opinion that whilst the Villages were doing a satisfactory job they had less onerous duties than some other masters and matrons with more populous workhouses to superintend.[11]

Although the Villages performed their duties to the satisfaction of the Aston Board, this does not mean that minor difficulties did not arise related to the way in which they ran the Workhouse. Workhouse life was undoubtedly restrictive and often oppressive for pauper inmates, but for officers cooped up in such institutions for most of the time, life was also rigidly structured, governed by rules and regulations and unrelenting routine. In such circumstances there was ample scope for petty disputes to develop between officers, and particular problems could arise between authoritarian masters and matrons and subordinate officers. Local workhouses were not immune from such problems, as illustrated by the strained relations between the Villages and successive schoolmistresses.[12]

The Aston Board appointed Miss Lilley, previously schoolmistress at the Birmingham Asylum for Infant Poor, as their first schoolmistress in May 1838. She was awarded a salary of £20 per annum, 'with her maintenance along with the Master and Matron in the House.' For a while all went smoothly and the Guardians expressed their satisfaction with her work. However, in January 1839, the Board became aware of tension between the Villages and Miss Lilley, and the Board chairman, Joseph Webster, was asked to arbitrate.[13]

Upon investigation Mr Webster discovered several points of contention between the Villages and Miss Lilley, differences he deemed 'trifling'. Thus Mr Village felt that the schoolmistress should take charge of the children's clean linen and attend to its mending. While Miss Lilley agreed to the former, she asserted that mending was best done by 'persons employed to get up the wash.' Mr Village was also concerned about the time at which Miss Lilley put out the fire in her apartment. She stated that she put the fire out carefully every night and expressed her readiness to extinguish it at any time required by the Guardians. That Miss Lilley should first secure his permission when she wished to go out of the Workhouse and the desirability of her assisting the matron in 'serving up dinner' were also amongst matters raised by Mr Village. For her part Miss Lilley commented that her duties had not been 'precisely defined' and that she had been doing 'in every respect what she believed to be right'. She also remarked that she was 'distressed by the irritating and often dictatorial language & manner of the Governor & Matron to her.'[14]

Mr Webster's report and recommendations, endorsed by the Guardians, sought to ease the tense relations between the Villages and Miss Lilley. Thus, it was confirmed that Miss Lilley 'was at liberty to go out at proper times,' but that she should ensure that the master and matron were informed in advance. It was also emphasised that involvement with the serving of dinner was not part of the schoolmistress' duties; the matron was to 'avail herself of all the assistance the inmates of the House could afford in the kitchen.' Once the duties of the various officers had been more clearly defined, Mr Webster felt that the Village's manner towards their fellow officers would 'be much softened'. In summing up his report, Mr Webster stated that he was satisfied that Miss Lilley was

> *well qualified by ability and acquirement, for the duties she has undertaken; and that the zeal with which she discharges them entitle her to our confidence. And at the same time the cleanliness order and good conduct shown in every part of the Union Workhouse reflect the highest credit on the Governor and Matron.*[15]

Although the Guardians were satisfied at the time that the problems between Miss Lilley and the Villages had been resolved, in April 1839 she resigned. The Guardians expressed their regret over her decision, but given that Mr Village had again written to the Guardians about her, it is clear that things had not improved.[16] Interestingly, Miss M A Burman, appointed as schoolmistress in June 1839, departed under similar circumstances. She was soon involved in a 'misunderstanding' with the matron over her duties and was clearly unhappy residing at the Workhouse. The Guardians tried to resolve the difficulties, but following their decision to deny Miss Burman permission to reside out of the Workhouse, she resigned in December 1839.[17] Another schoolmistress, Miss Jane Young, who was only in post from November 1846 until February 1847, may also have left abruptly because of tense relations with the Villages.[18]

Mr and Mrs Village remained in office until Lady Day 1848, when they retired, having expressed the view that 'in consequence of age and increasing infirmities,' [they would] soon be incapable of discharging the duties intrusted [sic] to them'. That the Guardians had continued to be satisfied with their performance is clear; much regret was expressed at their departure and they were given a glowing testimonial.[19]

Kings Norton Union Workhouse Masters and Matrons, 1836-50
The Tonks: Continuity, Retirement and Marriage

At the Kings Norton Union Workhouse, formerly the Kings Norton Parish Workhouse, the Kings Norton Board of Guardians retained the services of the existing master and matron following unionisation in 1836. John Tonks and his daughter Louisa continued as master and matron until 1839, with Miss Tonks remaining as matron until 1850. The Tonks were formally appointed in February 1837, at a joint salary of £60 per annum. Against a background of alterations to the Workhouse, Miss Tonks performed her duties to the full satisfaction of the Guardians and Assistant Commissioner Richard Earle. However, there was less satisfaction with the master, and it was decided not to increase their joint salary in March 1838. In his June 1838 quarterly report to the PLC, Mr Earle commented:

> *I cannot get rid of the old Master of the W.H. He is very incompetent, but the improvement of the House not being complete he has found it hitherto in his power to assign that as an excuse for those irregularities of which I have complained.*[20]

In December 1838, however, Mr Tonks decided to resign. Whether he resigned under pressure is unclear, but the Guardians did not try to persuade him to stay and in his December quarterly report to the PLC Assistant Commissioner Weale, referring to his imminent departure, reiterated that he was 'quite unfit for his situation'. Unusually, given that masters and matrons were generally expected to be married couples, there appears to have been no question that Miss Tonks should remain as matron, and the Guardians promptly advertised for 'a single middle aged man as Governor of the Workhouse'. His salary was to be £40 per annum, with Miss Tonks' salary set at £30 per annum. Subsequently William Benton, a Birmingham widower 'without incumbrance [sic]', was appointed to the vacancy.[21]

Unfortunately the new master soon proved unsatisfactory. At the beginning of June 1839, the Guardians censured Mr Benton for 'permitting the paupers to leave the House without the authority of the Board' and he was enjoined 'strictly to enforce and act upon the instructions of the Poor Law Commissioners in the management and Governance of the Workhouse and its inmates.' In the presence of Assistant Commissioner Weale, the Board accepted Mr Benton's resignation at the end of July. It is not unreasonable to assume that his early departure was hastened by pressure from the Guardians and the PLC.[22]

Following Mr Benton's resignation, it was again decided to appoint a new master and retain Miss Tonks' services. A Kings Norton man, William Phillips, was subsequently appointed at the agreed salary of £40 per annum plus 'the Usual allowance of Provisions'. Interestingly, by October 1839 Miss Tonks had married William Phillips. Whether the couple married for love or simply for convenience is unclear, but the Guardians were not unhappy as they were able to reduce their joint salary from £70 to £60 a year.[23]

The Phillips Scandal

The Phillips held office for a decade, until a scandal led to their sudden departure. In November 1850, a pauper called Ann Palmer, who had recently given birth to an illegitimate child, came before the Board and stated that Mr Phillips was the baby's father. Having made further inquiries, the Guardians decided that the allegations warranted an official investigation by Inspector Weale. After a thorough investigation, Mr Weale concluded that although it was a 'matter of some doubt ' whether William Phillips was the child's father, he had certainly 'had at different times sexual connexion [sic]' with Ann Palmer.[24]

Presumably to avoid further embarrassment, Mr Phillips tendered his resignation in December 1850. He asserted that the charges against him were completely false and protested his innocence, but stated that in view of his wife's illness and the difficulty of continuing to carry out his duties he felt that it was best to resign. The Guardians accepted the Phillips' resignation and, having consulted with Mr Weale, the PLB swiftly endorsed their decision.[25]

Birmingham Workhouse Governors and Matrons, 1830-44
The Alcocks: Death in Office

Mr and Mrs Thomas Alcock were governor and matron of the old Birmingham Workhouse in Lichfield Street from 1830-40. (Figure 3) Following the death in office of the previous governor, in June 1829, Mr Alcock, the House clerk, was temporarily appointed to the office. His appointment as governor, and that of his wife as matron, was confirmed in April 1830, at a joint salary of £200 per annum, plus

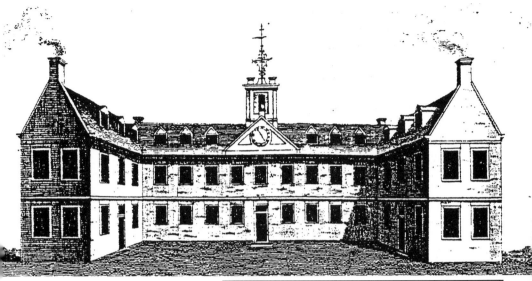

Figure 3. The 'Old' Birmingham Workhouse, Lichfield Street. *Birmingham Reference Library.*

£50 per annum in consideration of Mr Alcock's continuance as House clerk. In 1836, following the resignation of the previous post holders, the Guardians also appointed Mr Alcock as governor of the separate Asylum for Infant Poor (without any addition to his salary), with his daughter as matron. They held these appointments until the spring of 1838, when the Guardians decided that a married couple ought to be in charge of the Asylum.[26]

It is probable that the extra responsibilities placed upon Mr Alcock took their toll and hastened his death in office in October 1840. After his death, Mr Alcock received fulsome praise from the Guardians, the Minutes stating that they desired:

> to record their sense of the value of the character of the deceased Governor…, and the high estimation of the efficiency and diligence with which he discharged the arduous duties of his situation, which was characterized by industry and perseverance, firmness and

Figure 4. Bank note issued by the 'Old' Birmingham Workshouse. *Birmingham Reference Library.*

> *humanity, by which he obtained the respect of the Guardians, and the Rate Payers in General, while he secured the confidence and regard of the Poor under his charge.*

Although the Guardians had recognised Mr Alcock's abilities and expressed their appreciation of his work, like their counterparts elsewhere they had not been averse to saving money on salaries and adding still further to his already onerous responsibilities.[27] (Figure 4)

The Clarkes: The Consequences of Incompetence

After Mr Alcock's death, as was generally the case in such circumstances, Mrs Alcock resigned and the Board appointed William Clarke and his wife Rebecca as the new governor and matron in November 1840, at a joint salary of £150 a year. Selected from a field of twenty-seven applicants, they were considered to be 'well qualified', having had previous experience as governor and matron of workhouses in London and Oxford. Mr Clarke was fifty-five, whilst his wife was fifty-eight, and they had no dependant children, always a bonus to cost conscious Guardians.[28]

Unfortunately, the Clarkes did not fulfil the Guardians' expectations. In April 1842, the House Committee informed the Board that 'after much patient forbearance' they felt that it was their duty to report that the Workhouse was not being 'efficiently conducted', and that 'the ages of the parties and their fixed habits' militated against an improvement in the way the Clarkes fulfilled their duties. Under these circumstances, the Clarkes decided to resign rather than face possible dismissal for incompetence, and the Guardians readily accepted this.[29]

The Hirst Scandal

In June 1842, the Board appointed the Clarkes' replacements. From the ten applications received, five couples were considered for appointment; of these, three were already Board employees, whilst another couple were employed by the Wolverhampton Guardians. However, in a ballot the Board selected the fifth couple, Mr and Mrs Godfrey Swift Hirst, Anglicans who had been married for seven years, were aged forty and thirty-three respectively and had no children, and who were also able to commence their duties as soon as required.[30]

Appointed at a joint salary of £150 per annum plus board and lodging, only eighteen months later the Hirsts were engulfed in a major scandal. In November 1843, the PLC received an anonymous letter containing serious allegations about Mr Hirst's conduct. As a result the PLC, keen to assert more control over Poor Law administration in Birmingham, despatched Assistant Commissioner Weale to investigate.[31]

The most serious allegation made against Mr Hirst was that he had

> *confined 4 Boys for 8 days and nights in the Black hole, and kept them on water Gruel all the time and in a complete state of nudity without even a Shirt even to cover their nakedness or shelter them from the inclemency of the weather;* [that] *they became ill from their treatment* [and] *that the Surgeon was obliged to be called in to them.*

He was said to have found them 'in a horrible plight walking in their own filth.' A second allegation was that Mr Hirst had since placed 'a little Boy' in the 'hole', and that following his ordeal it had been necessary for him to 'be put in a warm Bath and wraped [sic] in Blankets to bring him about.' Thirdly, it was alleged that Mr Hirst had had a young woman called Rodders removed from the Infirmary and put into the Tramp Room as a 'punishment'. Lastly, it was alleged that a man called Bates had been taken from another ward and placed 'into a Cell in the Insane Wards for punishment.' In addition, the anonymous correspondent also commented that Mr Hirst drank 'spirits to an excess daily.' Most emotively, in calling for a PLC enquiry, the writer remarked that an enquiry 'into this horrid treatment' of paupers by Mr Hirst would 'serve the public but more particularly the poor who are so unfortunate to fall into the hands of such a Barbarian.'[32]

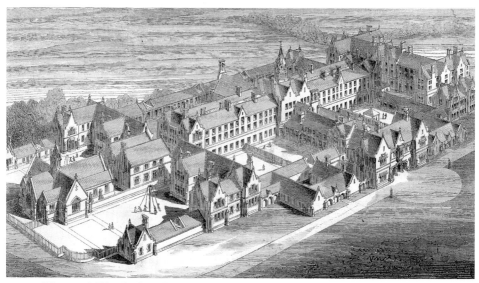

Figure 5. Birmingham New Workhouse. *Birmingham Reference Library.*

Mr Weale presided over a very thorough enquiry at the Workhouse. A large number of individuals, including Mr Hirst, were required to give evidence and

> *statements were elicited tending to show that transactions corresponding in character with those specified... would appear to have taken place.*[3] (Figures 5 and 6)

In their report on the matter to the Guardians on 2 January 1844, the House Committee, although it expressed annoyance over the PLC's intervention, recommended that the Guardians should investigate

Figure 6. Plan of Birmingham Workhouse. *Birmingham Reference Library.*

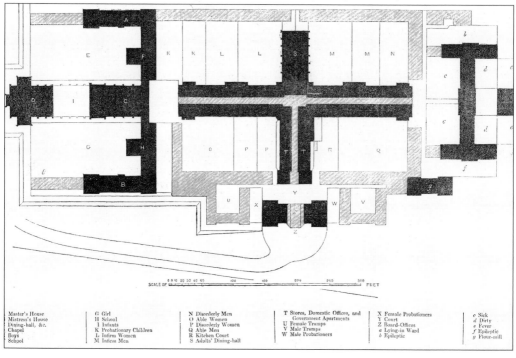

SCALE OF FEET

Master's House	G Girl	N Disorderly Men	T Stores, Domestic Offices, and	X Female Probationers
Mistress's House	H School	O Able Women	Government Apartments	Y Court
Dining-hall, &c.	I Infants	P Disorderly Women	U Female Tramps	Z Board-Offices
Chapel	K Probationary Children	Q Able Men	V Male Tramps	z Lying-in Ward
Boys	L Infirm Women	R Kitchen Court	W Male Probationers	b Epileptic
School	M Infirm Men	S Adults' Dining-hall		

c Sick	
d Dirty	
e Fever	
f Epileptic	
g Flour-mill	

further themselves. The House Committee were unable to deny that there were problems at the Workhouse, and had acknowledged as much to Mr Weale, but they had also sought to excuse Mr Hirst for over-zealousness. Thus it was remarked:

> *the Committee has been led to fear that on some occasions, he has exercised his authority in too arbitrary a manner, but for which the difficulty of controlling such an establishment may be an admissible excuse.*

The Guardians directed a special committee to investigate further and monitor any additional steps taken by the PLC.[34]

Events were now moving swiftly towards a confrontation between the PLC and the Guardians. Having received a damning report from Mr Weale, the PLC, eager to assert its authority *vis-à-vis* the Birmingham Board, issued Orders for the dismissal of the Hirsts on 4 January, as well as new Workhouse rules and regulations. Jealously protective of their rights and privileges under the terms of the 1831 local Act, the Guardians were thereby provoked into challenging the PLC's authority to dismiss officers they had appointed under the terms of that Act. In outright defiance of the PLC, the Guardians decided that the Hirsts should continue in office. A re-constituted special committee was charged with monitoring further PLC communications, seeking legal opinion as to the PLC's powers in respect of Board officers and consideration of the new rules and regulations. However, the committee was also empowered to make further investigations into Mr Hirst's conduct.[35]

Subsequently, on 2 February, the special committee reported that they had re-considered all the evidence and re-questioned Mr Hirst and others. The outcome of which was that they now recommended his immediate dismissal. In view of the seriousness of the proven charges against him, the Guardians could no longer place their confidence in Mr Hirst. It had been established that four 'Tramps' Jones, Blyth, Carter and Young, had been detained on the orders of Mr Hirst in inhuman conditions for ten days and nights, and that he had not visited them during that period. Compounding this, another tramp called John Delaney had also subsequently been treated in a similar way. Consequently, the committee asserted that Mr Hirst's dismissal was 'imperatively called for'; although regret was expressed that the services of Mrs Hirst would have to be dispensed with, as she was deemed to be 'industrious, attentive to her duties, intelligent, and very kindly disposed towards the Poor under her care.' The Board concurred with the committee's view and on 7 February, the

Hirsts' dismissal was confirmed.[36]

Although the Guardians had now fallen into line with the PLC's wishes, in view of the overwhelming evidence against Mr Hirst, the PLC had been prepared to pursue the matter very forcefully with or without the Guardians' co-operation. While the Guardians stalled over the Hirsts' dismissal, Mr Weale kept the PLC fully informed of developments and pressure for their removal from office was maintained.[37]

The PLC was well satisfied with the outcome of the Hirst scandal, vindicating as it did their stance and strengthening their influence over the Birmingham Guardians' affairs. Evident delight in the Guardians' volte-face was displayed by Mr Weale in a letter to the PLC of 6 February. With it he enclosed a letter from one of the pro-PLC Guardians, David Malins, of which Mr Weale commented: 'it will I think amuse you.' In his letter Mr Malins satirically referred to the special committee's discovery that 'the case is so much more heinous than the one investigated by the *secret, ex-parte* tribunal of the Commissioner [sic]

> and the fact that it had not hesitated in recommending Mr Hirsts' immediate dismissal. On a more serious note he also made reference to the opposition of many Guardians to the PLC and its directives, and remarked that he himself had been 'snubbed as the Commissioners' agent.'[38]

Conclusion

While every officer's case was different, overall the experience of the Birmingham, Aston and Kings Norton Workhouse masters and matrons during the 1830s and 40s reflects the wider national picture. Like their counterparts elsewhere they had a difficult job to do, subject to a multitude of pressures and demands. Their salary levels were closely controlled and workhouse life spawned tensions with other officers. Some individuals proved unequal to the demands of their job and some died in office. Others succumbed to the temptations of office and abused their position of authority.

As far as the Birmingham Workhouse masters and matrons are concerned, the tense relations between the Guardians and the PLC were always in the background during the 1840s. Staffing issues of all kinds, but especially disciplinary cases and most notably the Hirst scandal, were an important avenue via which the PLC and subsequently the PLB gradually extended their influence over Parish affairs from the 1840s onwards.

Notes and References

1. Tolley P.L., *Poor Relief and the Urban Poor. The Birmingham Guardians and the Administration of Indoor Relief in the Parish of Birmingham, during the early New Poor Law Era, c1830-1860*. CNAA MA Coventry (Lanchester) Polytechnic, 1987; Tolley P.L., *The Birmingham, Aston and Kings Norton Boards of Guardians, and the Politics and Administration of the Poor Law, circa 1836-1912*. Ph D De Montfort University, 1994.

2. See Crowther M.A., *The Workhouse System 1834-1929: The history of an English social institution*, Methuen, 1983; Gutchen R.M., Masters of workhouses under the new Poor Law, *Local Historian*, 16, 1984, pp 93-99.

3. See Anstruther I., *The Scandal of the Andover Workhouse*, Alan Sutton, 1984; Crowther, *The Workhouse System*, pp 31-32, 114, 118-23, 133-34 & 212-13; Digby A., The Rural Poor Law, in Fraser D (ed), *The New Poor Law in the Nineteenth Century*, Macmillan, 1976, p161; Gutchen, Masters of workhouses; Harling P., The Power of Persuasion: Central Authority, Local Bureaucracy and the New Poor Law, *English Historical Review*, 107, Jan 1992, p 35; Roberts D, How Cruel was the Victorian Poor Law? *Historical Journal*, 6 (1) 1963, pp 98 & 102.

4. Birmingham Reference Library (BRL): 23 Geo.III, Cap.liv, 1783; BRL: 1 & 2 Wm.IV, Cap.lxvii, 1831. The Parishes of St. Philip's, St.Martin's and St. George's were combined into a single Parish of Birmingham for poor relief purposes. McNaulty M., *Some Aspects of the History of the Administration of the Poor Laws in Birmingham between 1730 and 1834*. MA University of Birmingham, 1942, p 6. See also 4th *Annual Report of the Poor Law Commissioners for England and Wales*, 1838, pp 3-4; *8th Annual Report of the Poor Law Commissioners for England and Wales, 1842*, p 18; Ashforth D, The Urban Poor Law, in Fraser (ed), *The New Poor Law*, p 128; Crocker R H, The Victorian Poor Law in Crisis and Change: Southampton, 1870-, *Albion*, 19 (1) Spring 1987, pp 19-44; F. Driver, *Power and Pauperism: The workhouse system*, 1834-1884, Cambridge U P, 1993, pp 42-45; Forsythe W.J., Paupers and Policy Makers in Exeter 1830-1860. *Reports & Transactions Devonshire Association for the Advancement of Science*, 117, Dec 1985, pp 151-60; Searby P., The Relief of the Poor in Coventry, 1830-1863. *Historical Journal*, 20 (2) Jun 1977, pp 345-61.

5. BRL: Birmingham Guardians Minutes, 21.7.1909, 16.2.1910 & 1.4.1912; BRL: Aston Union Orders, 1836-57, Orders 12.10.1836 & 22.10.1836; Public Record Office (PRO): MH 12/14057, Order 10.1.1884; PRO: MH 33/2; 3rd Annual Report of the Poor Law Commissioners for England and Wales, 1837, pp 272 & 274; Showell W., *Dictionary of Birmingham*, S.R. Publishers, 1969 (Reprint of 1885 ed), p 246; Vince C.A., *History of the Corporation of Birmingham*, Vol IV (1900-1915), Cornish, 1923, pp 32 & 43.

6. 1st Annual Report of the Poor Law Commissioners for England and Wales, 1835, pp 101-04; BRL: Birmingham Orders, 1837-62, Order 24.7.1847. See also Gutchen, Masters of workhouses, p 96.

7. BRL: B. Orders, 1837-62, Orders 4.1.1844 & 16.1.1850. The PLC also issued workhouse rules and regulations orders to the Coventry and Exeter local Act Poor Law authorities in 1844. Forsythe, Paupers and Policy Makers in Exeter, p 158; Searby, The Relief of the Poor in Coventry, p 354.

8. BRL: B. Min., 2.6.1818 & 22.5.1822; BRL: Regulations for Conducting the Affairs of the Birmingham Workhouse, 1822; BRL: Rules and Regulations of the Guardians of the Poor of the Parish of Birmingham, 1841.

9. *Birmingham Gazette*, 2.11.1840, 6.6.1842 & 12.2.1844.

10. BRL: Aston Guardians Minutes, 18.9.1838, 2.10.1838 & 16.10.1838; PRO: MH 12/13233, letter Pearson E to PLC, 31.12.1841 & note Weale R to PLC, 5.1.1842. See also Brundage A., The English Poor Law of 1834 and the Cohesion of Agricultural Society, *Agricultural History*, 48 (3) Jul 1974, p 412; Crowther, *The Workhouse System*, p 116; Harling P., The Power of Persuasion, pp 35-36; Midwinter E.C., *Social Administration in Lancashire 1830-1860: Poor Law, Public Health and Police*, Manchester University Press, 1969, p 40.

11. BRL: A. Min., 15.5.1838, 5.6.1838, 2.10.1838, 27.11.1838, 18.12.1838, 16.3.1841, 28.9.1841, 7.12.1841, 21.12.1841 & 28.12.1841; PRO: MH 12/13233, letter Pearson E. to PLC, 31.12.1841, note Weale R. to PLC, 5.1.1842 & letter PLC to Pearson E., 15.1.1842. See also Crowther, *The Workhouse System*, pp 123-24; Dunkley P., The 'Hungry Forties' and the New Poor Law: A Case Study. *Historical Journal*, XVII (2) 1974, pp 341-43.

12. See Crowther, *The Workhouse System*, pp 114-15 & 130-33; Digby A., *Pauper Palaces*, Routledge & Kegan Paul, 1978, pp 187-88; Gutchen, Masters of workhouses, p 98; Rochester M., *The Northwich Poor Law Union & Workhouse*, Cheshire Libraries and Museums, 198?.

13. BRL: A. Min., 1.5.1838, 8.5.1838, 26.6.1838 & 1.1.1839; BRL: B. Min., 3.8.1837, 11.4.1838 & 18.4.1838.

14. BRL: A. Min., 15.1.1839 & 22.1.1839.

15. *Ibid.*, 22.1.1839.
16. *Ibid.*, 16.4.1839 & 23.4.1839.
17. *Ibid.*, 18.6.1839, 15.10.1839, 5.11.1839, 17.12.1839, 24.12.1839 & 31.12.1839.
18. *Ibid.*, 17.11.1846 & 23.2.1847.
19. *Ibid.*, 21.9.1847, 5.10.1847 & 21.11.1848. See also Crowther, *The Workhouse System*, pp 119 & 125.
20. BRL: Kings Norton Guardians Minutes, 10.2.1837 & 23.3.1838; PRO: MH 32/21, Quarterly report Earle R to PLC, 30.6.1838.
21. BRL: K.N. Min., 14.12.1838, 4.1.1839 & 8.2.1839; PRO: MH 32/85, Quarterly report Weale R. to PLC, 31.12.38; PRO: MH 12/14039, letter Docker R. to PLC, 5.3.1839, note Weale R. to PLC, 7.3.1839 & letter PLC to Docker R., 8.3.1839; *Gazette*, See also Crowther, *The Workhouse System*, pp 116-17 & 119-20; Harling P., The Power of Persuasion, pp 36-37 & 46-47.
22. BRL: K.N. Min., 14.6.1839 & 26.7.1839. See also Crowther, *The Workhouse System*, pp 119-20.
23. BRL: K.N. Min., 2.8.1839, 30.8.1839, 25.10.1839, 20.12.1839 & 1.5.1840. See also Crowther, *The Workhouse System*, pp 121 & 123-24; Wood P., *Poverty and the Workhouse in Victorian Britain*, Alan Sutton, 1991, p 91.
24. BRL: K.N. Min., 20.11.1850 & 4.12.1850; PRO: MH 12/14041, note Weale R. to PLB, 31.12.1850.
25. BRL: K.N. Min., 18.12.1850; PRO: MH 12/14041, letter Docker R. to PLB, 24.12.1850, letter Phillips W. to K.N. Guardians, 18.12.1850 & letter PLB to Docker R, 3.1.1851.
26. BRL: B. Min., 30.6.1829, 27.4.1830, 5.10.1836, 7.12.1836 & 18.4.1838; *Gazette* Birmingham's first Workhouse, situated in Lichfield Street was erected in 1733/34 and subsequently extended. The new Workhouse on Birmingham Heath did not open until 1852. The Asylum for Infant Poor in Summer Lane, a separate institution for the care of child paupers, was opened by the Overseers and Guardians in 1797. (See Royal Commission on the Poor Laws, 1834, Appendix B2, Answers to Town Queries, p 239g, 24; Dent R K, *The Making of Birmingham: Being A History of the Rise and Growth of the Midland Metropolis*, Allday J.L., and Simpkin, Marshall and Co, 1894, pp 75 & 431-32; Dent R K, *Old and New Birmingham: a history of the town and its people*, E.P. Publishing, 1973 (Reprint of 1878-80 publication), pp 500-01; Gill C., *History of Birmingham, Vol I: Manor and Borough to 1865*, Oxford U P, 1952, p 150; Hutton W, *An History of Birmingham*, E.P. Publishing, 1976 (Reprint of 1783 ed.), pp 216-17; Langford J.A.(ed.), *Modern Birmingham and its Institutions: a chronicle of local events, from 1841 to 1871, Vol 1 (to 1861)*, Osborne E.C., and Simpkin, Marshall & Co, 1873, pp 381-83; McNaulty, *Some Aspects of the History of the Administration of the Poor Laws in Birmingham*, pp 21-24; Upton C., *A History of Birmingham*, Phillimore, 1993, p 40.
27. BRL: B. Min., 13.10.1840. See also Crowther, *The Workhouse System*, pp 119 & 125.
28. BRL: B. Min., 13.10.1840, 23.11.1840 & 5.1.1841. See also Crowther, *The Workhouse System*, pp 116-17.
29. BRL: B. Min., 5.4.1842, 13.4.1842 & 2.5.1842; Gazette, 9.5.1842. See also Rochester, *The Northwich Poor Law Union*.
30. BRL: B. Min., 22.6.1842; Gazette, 27.6.1842. See also Crowther, *The Workhouse System*, p 117.
31. BRL: B. Min., 22.6.1842 & 2.1.1844.
32. *Ibid.*, 2.1.1844.
33. *Ibid.*, 2.1.1844; *Gazette*, 27.11.1843 & 11.12.1843; Birmingham Journal, 2.12.1843, 9.12.1843 & 16.12.1843.
34. BRL: B. Min., 2.1.1844; *Journal*, 6.1.1844.
35. BRL: B. Min., 10.1.1844 & 15.1.1844; BRL: B. Orders, 1837-62, Order 4.1.1844; PRO: MH 12/13288, letter Bynner W. to Chadwick E., 6.1.1844 & letter Bynner W. to Chadwick E., 7.1.1844; *Journal*, 13.1.1844 & 20.1.1844. See also Crowther, *The Workhouse System*, pp 121-22.
36. BRL: B. Min., 2.2.1844 & 7.2.1844.
37. PRO: MH 12/13288, letter Weale R. to PLC, 12.1.1844, extract from the *Midland Counties Herald*, 11.1.1844, letter PLC to Weale R., 15.1.1844, letter PLC to Bynner W., 19.1.1844 & letter Bynner W. to Chadwick E., 20.1.1844.
38. *Ibid.*, letter Weale R. to PLC, 6.2.1844 & letter Malins D. to Weale R., 3.2.1844.

2. SOME LESSER KNOWN CHARACTERS OF BIRMINGHAM

by Patrick Baird

MOST PEOPLE KNOW ABOUT the famous personalities of Birmingham, such as Matthew Boulton, James Watt, John Baskerville, the Cadbury family and Joseph and Neville Chamberlain. There are many others who ought to be brought to the public's attention but very seldom are. This article includes some of those who, for various reasons, add to the variety of Birmingham life.

Jane Bunford 1895-1922

In the 1970s the name of the above became well known following an item on the ITV programme *Midlands Today*. Up until then she had been known to only a few except members of her own family. She in fact suffered from gigantism and the television programme suggested that after death her body had been 'snatched' and had been handed over to Birmingham University for research.

But to go back to the beginning – Jane was born at Bartley Green on 26 July 1895. Her father was a metal caster and she was one of seven children. She attended St Michael's School but before she had been there very long it was evident that all was not well. Jane was growing much taller than any of her classmates.

She was withdrawn from school at the age of thirteen, her height now making it awkward and uncomfortable for her to continue. She eventually attained a height of seven feet nine inches, thus becoming the tallest woman the world had ever known. Residents who knew her recall her cleaning the upstairs windows of their cottage in Jiggins Lane while standing on the ground.

Naturally she was embarrassed by her height and stayed indoors during daylight, though her niece remembered her going to her house further up Jiggins Lane on Saturday evenings to look after her when her parents went to the theatre. Jane possessed unusual copper-coloured hair which, when loose, fell about her like a cloak, reaching to her ankles. On more than one occasion offers to buy her hair were made to her, as were others asking her to appear in shows, which were of course refused. Meantime she developed a talent for embroidery.

She died on 1 April 1922 of Hyperpituitarism and Gigantism. She was buried in St Michael's Churchyard at Bartley Green and her coffin measured eight feet two inches in length.

The apparent mystery in later years stems from the fact that the Anatomical Museum at Birmingham University displayed in the 1970s a skeleton, seven feet nine inches in length asserted to have been that of a Northfield woman who died in 1922 but the University had no record of the deceased or the donation of the remains.

This gave rise on the television programme to an insinuation of body snatching to which there is no evidence whatsoever. From brothers and sisters of Jane still alive at this period the truth emerged. They had memories of their father presenting the body to the museum that then skeletonised it and returned the remains for burial. Jane's burial took place four days after her death so it was quite possible that this is what occurred.

Just on a further note. In the early nineteenth century there lived in Birmingham a Viennese born woman Nanette Stocker, who became known as the female 'Tom Thumb', only thirty-three inches high. She now lies buried in St Philips Churchyard.

George Dixon 1820-1898

Educational reformer who was born on the 1 July 1820 at Gomersal, near Bradford in Yorkshire. He was the son of Abraham Dixon of Whitehaven. Soon after his birth his father moved to Leeds and on the 26 January 1829 George entered Leeds Grammar School. In 1838 he moved to Birmingham and began working for Raybone Brothers and Company, Foreign Merchants. In 1844 he was made a partner and ultimately on the retirement of his brother Abraham he became head of the firm. In connection with the business he also spent three years in Australia. (Figure 1)

After his return he became involved with municipal affairs. He was an active member of the Birmingham and Edgbaston Debating Society, in which almost all local politicians learned and practised the art of speaking. He embarked on several undertakings with a view to improving the condition of the people. Mainly owing to his efforts, Aston Hall and Park was

Figure 1. George Dixon.
Birmingham Reference Library..

secured for the town and he was also one of the original promoters of the Rifle Volunteer Movement in Birmingham, which was inaugurated at a meeting held in a Committee Room of the town Hall in December 1859.

In 1863 he was elected Councillor for Edgbaston Ward and on the 9 November 1866 he was elected Mayor. His year of office was memorable for the riots in June 1867 occasioned by the anti-popery propaganda of the zealots named William Murphy and of George Hammond Whalley. It was necessary to call out a squadron of hussars to disperse the mob, and Dixon, who had previously refused Murphy the use of the town Hall, rode boldly among the enraged crowd in the Bull Ring and read the *Riot Act*.

Dixon, who was an advanced liberal in politics, took an active interest in the question of popular education. Early in 1867 he initiated a series of conferences on the state of education in Birmingham, which were attended by representatives of all political parties and of various shades of religious thought. The conference passed a resolution that it was desirable to promote an act of parliament 'empowering municipal corporations to levy a rate for educational purposes', and another deprecating the employment of children of young age, unless due provision was made for their instruction at school. A third resolution advocating compulsory education, in which Dixon was supported by Joseph Chamberlain, found the Society divided in opinion. These conferences led to the formation of the Birmingham Education Aid Society, to provide additional schools and to pay fees of poor children.

In 1868, with the co-operation of Chamberlain, John Sandford, George Dawson and Robert William Dale, the national Education League was founded at a private meeting at Dixon's residence. It had for its object 'the establishment of the system which should secure the education of every child in England and Wales', and carried out active propaganda throughout the country. The first conference of the League was held in Birmingham on the 12 and 13 October 1869 when Dixon filled the office of President.

On the death of William Scholefield, Dixon was elected to Parliament for Birmingham on the 23 July 1867. On the introduction of the Elementary Education Bill by William Edward Forster in 1870, George took a leading part in endeavouring to amend it in accordance with the views of the advanced liberals. He moved an amendment to the second reading, opposing the proposal to leave the question of religious instruction to be determined by local authorities. The amendment was rejected after a long debate.

On 5 March 1872 he unsuccessfully moved a resolution in condemnation of the *Elementary Education Act*, chiefly because it omitted to provide for the general establishment of School Boards, and in 1874 he assisted with bringing in a Bill to make compulsory attendance general, which was supported by Forster, but not passed. Dixon was elected to the first Birmingham School Board on 28 November 1870 and was re-elected in 1873 and 1876 when he retired from Parliament due to the ill health of his wife.

In 1885 when the boundaries of the parliamentary borough of Birmingham were extended Dixon was elected for the Edgbaston division, a seat that he retained until his death in 1898. On 4 January 1898 Dixon received the honorary freedom of Birmingham from the City Council and just twenty days later he died at his residence, 'The Dales', at Edgbaston. He was buried in Witton Cemetery on 28 January.

He married in 1855, Mary, youngest daughter of James Stansfeld, Judge of the Halifax County Court, and sister of Sir James Stansfeld, She died on 25 March 1885, leaving three sons and three daughters.

John Jaffray 1818-1901

John Jaffray, the founder of the *Birmingham Post* and the Jaffray Hospital at Erdington was born at Stirling in Scotland in 1818 and was educated at Glasgow High School. He came to England as a reporter on a newspaper at Shrewsbury and came to Birmingham in 1844 to take up a post on the *Birmingham Journal*, offered to him by the newspaper's proprietor, John Feeney. Jaffray proved to have such a good business brain as well as literary power that Feeney decided to make him a partner in the newspaper and an agreement between them was drawn up in 1852. Within a few years Jaffray began to make his mark in the town as a businessman and public figure. (Figure 2)

Everything he did was marked with the sign of success and there was no movement in Birmingham, whether it was connected to politics, the arts and literature or philanthropy, to which he did not belong. In 1857 he helped Feeney found the newspaper the *Birmingham Daily Post*, later shortened to the *Birmingham Post*.

Figure 2. John Jaffray.
Birmingham Reference Library.

By the time he died in 1901 he had accumulated a great deal of wealth, had become a Baronet and had acquired the tastes and possessions of an aristocratic country squire, having bought a mansion that stood in acres of ground just off Bristol Road, next to where King Edward's School now stands – an independent school.

Perhaps his most major philanthropic works was to have built and equip the Jaffray Hospital in Erdington, which stood in eight acres of grounds. It was opened by the Prince of Wales, later Edward VII, on 29 November 1885 as a place where the helpless would be properly looked after and brought back to good health.

Henry Jones 1811-1914

At the age of one hundred Henry Jones was still active in the field of gun making. He had always been an excellent workman and for years he was reckoned amongst the most skilful craftsmen in the trade, and in his time he produced a number of epoch making improvements in the construction of firearms.

As far back as 1835 he invented the first self-acting revolver, and again in 1868 he laid the gun trade under a lasting obligation by his improvements in the mechanism of the breechloader.

At this great age of one hundred he was working on two other inventions, from one of which, a device for preventing firearms exploding prematurely, he anticipated great things. Unfortunately, notwithstanding his exceptional skill, he could not regard himself as a wealthy man. Although his inventions brought almost untold wealth to Birmingham they brought him no great monetary advantage.

Regarding his first great invention, he used to tell an amusing story. His father, Mr Charles Jones, who at one time was in partnership with Sir Edward Thomason, the eminent jeweller and medallist, conceived the idea of bringing the new self acting pocket pistol, as it was called, before the naval and military authorities of the day. Henry arranged to give a lecture on 'Some recent improvements in gun mechanism' at the Polytechnic in London. This was in 1835. The room was filled with representative officers from both arms of the service and at the close of the lecture, in the course of which the main features of the revolver were fully explained, the weapon itself was handed round, and so great was the interest created that orders for £700 worth of pistols were booked immediately.

As the lecturer was on the point of leaving, an American gentleman approached and offered to buy the specimen pistol he held in his hand just as it stood. Mr Jones did not wish to part with it, so he put what he thought was a prohibitive price on it – fifteen guineas. To his great astonishment and confusion the American promptly put his hand in his pocket, counted out the money, and took the revolver.

The weapon today is of no practical interest although at the time it was looked upon as an important invention. Formerly, the nearest approach to it was the 'four shot' pistol, made chiefly in West Bromwich – a crude arrangement in which the barrel containing the four shots had to be rotated by hand. Jones conceived the idea of rendering the rotation automatic on movement of the trigger, and after a few experiments succeeded in carrying it out successfully.

Who the American was and what he did with the revolver we do not know but one concludes that the transaction had a serious and sinister effect on Jones's own fortunes.

The breech loader mechanism was a much more important mechanism, and came about somewhere around 1858. Prior to that time there had been many attempts made to produce breech-loading weapons, some of them dating back to the time of Henry VIII, but so far they had failed because of some weakness at the breech. One of the most successful implements of this type was one designed by a Parisian gunsmith named Lefaucheux in 1836. Jones's invention followed similar lines, but was carried out in a more practical fashion. The lever fitted over the trigger guard and the pivot had two projections instead of one. It not only afforded a double grip but also drew the barrels down to the bed of the breech and held them securely so that there would be no movement and consequently, no escape of gas after the explosion.

Again he made very little money out of this. He had entered into an arrangement with a firm of gunmakers whereby the latter undertook to patent the invention and share the profits. They applied for and obtained provisional protection but unfortunately, somehow or other omitted to complete the patent, with the result that after a few short months the improvements became public property. Hence the man of genius who originated the mechanism remained comparatively poor and lost almost in obscurity, while the gunmakers reaped harvests of gold from his invention.

In an interview with the *Birmingham Mail* on his hundredth birthday he could not say exactly where he was born. 'It is so long ago that I cannot remember' he jokingly remarked. But he was probably born in an institution established by his father, a repository of the arts and sciences called the 'Pantechnetedra' in New Street near to Union Passage and after being educated in a school in

Westmoreland, he returned to Birmingham. At the time of his 100th birthday he lived at 13 Great King Street. He died in August 1914 at 26 Nursery Road, Hockley.

Alexander Parkes 1813-1890
An American inventor called John Wesley Hyatt (1837-1920) supposedly invented celluloid in 1868 and in 1895 two French brothers, Auguste and Louis Lumiere, built the world's first cinema and produced the first film news reels and the first motion picture in history. But it was Alexander Parkes who we should really thank for the invention of celluloid in 1855.

Alexander Parkes was the son of a Birmingham brass lock manufacturer, James Mears Parkes of Suffolk Street, where he was born on 29 December 1813.

As a young man he was apprenticed to a local brass founding firm, Messenger and Sons, and subsequently entered the service of Messrs Elkington, in whose works he had charge of the casting departments. His attention was soon directed to the subject of electro-plating, which was then being introduced by his employers and in 1841 he secured his first patent (no. 8905) for 'the Electro deposition of Works of Art'. In his early patents, Parkes described himself as an artist but later chose the more correct designation of 'chemist'.

Among the ingenious processes which he devised in connection with electro-metallurgy, mention should be made of his method of electro-plating flowers and fragile natural objects, which is included in a patent granted in 1843 (No. 9807). The objects are first dipped in a solution of phosphates in bisulphide of carbon and subsequently in nitrate of silver. A finely divided coating of silver is poured on to the specimen, upon which, when connected to a battery and placed in the proper solution, any quantity of copper, silver or gold can be deposited. On the occasion of a visit to Messrs Elkingtons' works, Prince Albert was presented with a spider's web which had been coated with silver.

Parkes was an exceedingly prolific inventor and his patents number sixty-six, extending over a period of forty-six years. In 1841 he patented a process for waterproofing fabrics by the use of a solution of india-rubber in bisulphide of carbon (No. 9807) which was used by Ethrington and Mason in Birmingham for some years, the patent being eventually sold to Macintosh and Co who then began to use the process for the production of 'Macs'.

From 1850 to 1853 Parkes was at Pembrey, South Wales, engaged in superintending the erection of copper-smelting works for

Ethington and Mason: and to this period belongs the method of using zinc for the desilverisation of lead which was first patented in 1850 (No. 13118) and further developed by patents granted in 1851 (No. 13673) and in 1852 (No. 13997). This process was used at Messrs Sims works at Llanelli until 1859, attracting much attention in Germany and was widely used in the USA.

During the Crimean War he had invented a new and infinitely more powerful powder than ordinary gunpowder which was suitable for small arms, cannons, shells or blasting purposes, and at his own expense exhibited this to the military personnel at a public trials on the sands at Burry Port, South Wales, on 17 August 1855. He used shells of thirteen inches and twenty-one inches diameter. He exploded these by means of a fuse. The effects of the explosion were terrific; some of the pieces being carried nearly a mile form the spot. The government, however, could not be induced to adopt the invention unless Mr Parkes would divulge the composition of the powder. This he did not think advisable to do and the matter went no further. He was strongly advised to offer it to the Russian or French governments but his patriotic feelings would not permit him to do so.

From 1854 to 1867 Parkes devoted a great amount of time in innumerable experiments, and at considerable expense, to improve the manufacture of Nitro-cellulose components so as to make it possible to use such agents in the production of a substitute he was about to introduce to take the place of India-rubber, Gutta-percha, Ivory and Tortoiseshell. When these experiments began, the cheapest form of Nitro-cellulose could only be obtained at about 10s (50p) or 12s (60p) per pound. But by the employment of machinery, and more especially by the use of various waste cotton products, in employing iron vessels for converting cotton or paper, by the means of acids, the use of iron agitators and iron vessels in pressing out the excess of acid by hydraulic pressure which could be used again after the addition of a certain proportion of new acid, he brought the price down to about 6d (2^{1}/2p) or 8d (3p).

This economy in the cost of pyroxyline and the introduction of castor oil and certain new solvents, such as vegetable Naphtha, Nitro-benzol, Camphor, etc enabled him to bring out his new material 'Parkesine', now known as celluloid which would eventually lead, unknown to him, to a thriving new industry – film making.

Parkesine formed the subject of a number of patents beginning in 1855 (No. 235) and continued to 1868. Articles made from the material were shown at the Universal Exhibition of 1862 in London and at the Paris Exhibition of 1867, both of which awarded him a medal.

Finding that markets were wanted for the use of 'Anthracite' or Stone Coal, of which there were immense deposits of excellent quality near Burry Port, Parkes gave his attention to the matter and discovered a method of burning it under the boilers of steam engines in smelting and other furnaces by introducing jets of steam under or through the fire bars (made hollow for the purpose). He did not have an opportunity of getting the method adopted and never derived any benefit from it, although it was later used very extensively.

Parkes left Birmingham about 1881 and went to reside at Bexley in Kent, later moving to West Dulwich where he died on 29 June 1890. He was buried in Norwood Cemetery.

Bibliography

All sources mentioned below can be found in the Local Studies and History Service, Birmingham Central Library.

Jane Bunford 1895-1922
1. Miscellaneous material relating to Jane Bunford 1895-1922.
  Catalogue number 669385.

George Dixon 1820-1898
1. *British National Biography*, Supplement Volume II, 1901.

John Jaffray 1818-1901
1. *Biography and Review*, Volume 3, 1880.
  Catalogue number 36456.
2. Arkinstall and Baird, *Erdington Past and Present*, 1976.
  Catalogue number 859301.

Henry Jones 1811-1914
1. *Birmingham Biography* News Cuttings, Volume 9, 1914-1916.
2. (Extracts from:-
    Birmingham Daily Mail, 21 August 1914.
    Birmingham Post, 21 August 1914.
    Birmingham Gazette, 22 August 1914.
    Birmingham Weekly Post, 29 August 1914.

Alexander Parkes 1813-1890
1. *A Short Memoir of Alexander Parkes, Chemist and Inventor*.
  Circa 1920. Printed for private circulation. Catalogue number 501660.
2. *Dictionary of National Biography*, Volume XLIII 1895.

3. THE PAGEANT OF BIRMINGHAM

by Richard Albutt

IN JANUARY 1938 ARTICLES started to appear in the Birmingham newspapers announcing that the 'General Purposes Committee of the City Council' was 'preparing for the celebration of the centenary of the granting of the charter of incorporation in Birmingham', and the celebrations would take place in July of that year. It is impossible to know how many people at the time actually knew what the charter was, but by the end of that summer very few locals could have been in any doubt at all.

Birmingham's Charter of Incorporation had arrived in the town on 1 November 1838 after a long struggle, begun in the April, by the presentation of a petition containing 8,700 signatures to the Privy Council. Local Tories had strongly disapproved claiming it was 'unnecessary' and 'not wanted', which led to months of protests and investigations before its final approval by Queen Victoria. Even after its announcement in the 'Court Circular' it took a month of anxious waiting before it made its actual appearance.

At a public reading of the Charter's more than 4,000 words, in the Town Hall on 5 November, R K Douglas described how the committee had been 'like Children waiting for a fairing, terribly impatient, and almost afraid it would not come at all' and how Mr Hutton had been 'twice to the railway to search for it. They told him the second time that it had probably gone on to Belfast'.[1] This perhaps says something about the way Birmingham was viewed by the government of the time but does not detract from the importance of this document, which enabled Birmingham to elect for the first time a Corporation consisting of a Mayor, sixteen Aldermen and forty-eight councillors.

One hundred years later the Council of the day felt that this centenary provided an important opportunity for a demonstration of civic pride, and the Lord Mayor, Councillor Canning, announced in a speech to the Consular Association that the main celebration 'would be an historical pageant at Aston Park' and that 'a committee of representative women of the city was needed to organise this event', which he hoped would involve at least 8,000 people.[2]

By the beginning of February the first steps towards realisation of this dream had been taken by the appointment of C E Elliot, organiser of the British Industries Fair, as Business manager and a 'Warwickshire woman', Gwen Lally, as director of this enormous extravaganza. Gwen Lally had considerable previous experience of pageants at Warwick, Runnymeade and Tewkesbury and this would be her thirteenth production. She was proudly claimed to be 'the only woman pageant master in the world'.

The Birmingham Amateur Dramatic Federation lent its support to the project and a mass meeting for interested parties was held at the Midland Institute on Wednesday, 16 February. Gwen Lally announced that 'the Centenary pageant to be produced in the grounds of Aston Hall next July is going to be the finest pageant of the era'. (Figure 1)

Mr S C Kaines Smith, Keeper of the Art Gallery, had agreed to write the scenario and gave an outline of the various scenes that would make up the performance. He obviously felt the need to

Figure 1. Pageant Headquarters in Cambridge Street. *Birmingham Reference Library.*

Figure 2. Ladies of the Victorian Era having trouble with their crinolines.
Birmingham Reference Library.

justify the inclusion of the Battle of Crecy as he stressed that,

> he had already ascertained from old records a list of thirty-eight
> members of society who had lived within the confines of the
> Birmingham of today and who fought in the battle of Crecy under
> their own arms... including two members of the De Bermingham
> family, and the lords of Weoley and Erdington which he felt made it
> very much a Birmingham battle.

He then appealed to

> the many who were not actors or who did not wish too take an active
> part in the pageant to spread the news that there was work to be done

for the honour and glory of the city that they all loved - clerical work and work behind the scenes.[3]

From this point on things gathered momentum and a series of fund raising events took place with Gwen Lally giving recruitment talks around the city, although remarkably she was at this time still directing 3,000 performers in an ice festival at Earls Court, and did not take up residency in Birmingham until 1 May. (Figure 2)

This activity met with some initial success, so that by the end of the month nearly 2,000 performers had been enrolled, however these were mostly female and men were less forthcoming. Over 1000 were required for the Battle of Crecy scene alone, so when things started to get desperate as rehearsals loomed large appeals where made for 'girls to bring along a boyfriend', and much was made of the fact that the King and Queen would be attending the celebrations.

Not everything went smoothly however, at a recruitment meeting in Yardley, cheers greeted a statement by J P Bridgwater that it was adding insult to injury for the City Council to say, although we are spoiling your district and acting entirely contrary to you strongly expressed wishes we want you to assist us in the celebration of our centenary.

This seems to have been a reference to the recent building of a housing estate on the meadows of Marshall Close.[4] There were also some complaints about the prices performers were expected to pay for their costumes. The *Evening Mail* reported:

A Handsworth reader declares that whereas costumes were supposed to cost 7s 6d, some performers are having to pay more than £1.

Then the charge for the seats, the writer goes on

how many people who would like to see the show can afford the top price of 12s 6d, The pageant is apparently for the upper ten... A Perry Barr critic points out that the majority of the 6,000 performers are only ordinary working people who are paying for their own costumes and giving their time freely and the added cost of travel will come very heavily on many.

The Pageant organisers were quick to reply:

It has been made perfectly clear at all the meetings in connection with the pageant that it would have to be self supporting and that consequently there must be a charge for costumes. It has been pointed out that as far as possible, it was hoped each performer would agree to bear the cost of his or her costume, which in the majority of cases,

Figure 3. The dinosaur outside the Town Hall. *Birmingham Reference Library.*
Figure 4. The dinosaur outside the *Cambridge Inn*. *Birmingham Reference Library.*

particularly where crowd costumes were concerned, would not exceed 5s or 7s 6d... The performers as a body are loyal volunteers who have gladly accepted these necessary conditions... It is suggested that the price of 2s 6d [including tax] for a reserve seat undercover is not excessive, while it must be remembered that there are about 1,350 side seats, which are not covered, at 1s 3d [including tax]. These are much the same prices as are charged at other pageants.

...With regard to transport arrangements for the performers, it has been decided that a flat rate of 4d for the return journey from anywhere inside the city, irrespective of distance, will be charged for performers during dress reversals and performances of the Pageant and this clearly represents a very substantial subsidy from the general pageant fund.[5]

In order to ease administration it was decided early on that the city would be divided into districts and each allocated a different scene to perform. These were:

Episode 1. **The prologue**, North East District: Erdington, Kingstanding, Saltley.

Episode 2. **The Market Charter**, South West District: Selly Oak, Kings Norton, Northfield, Bournville.

Episode 3. **The Battle of Crecy:** Central District.

Episode 4. **Aston Hall**, North District: Aston, Nechells, Lozells, Witton.

Episode 5. **The Restoration:** West District. Harborne, Rotton Park, Warley, Bartley Green, Edgbaston, Quinton.

Episode 6. **The Priestley Riots:** North West District. Handsworth, Winson Green, Perry Barr.

Episode 7. **The Visit of Queen Victoria.** East and South East District: Acocks Green, Adderley Park, Balsall Heath, Bordesley Green, Greet, Hall Green, Hay Mills, Kings Heath, Moseley, Shirley, Small Heath, Sparkbrook, Sparkhill, Stechford, Yardley, Yardley Wood.

This seems a rather disproportionate geographical area for the Victorian scene, particularly when it appears to have been one of the more popular episodes, with the opportunity to wear some attractive period costumes. The following appeal appeared in the *Evening Mail*:

Birmingham pageant organisers are searching for someone who measures a mere eighteen inches around the waist, to play the part of Queen Victoria. Miss Queen Lally, the pageant Master, is adamant about this measurement. She says 'The performer must not only fit the part but fit the costume as well' – Miss Jean Campbell [Mistress of the Robes] has an exact description of what the Queen wore when she visited Birmingham in 1858 – a dress of grey barege trimmed with plaid. But someone must be found to fit it.

An American girl, Jeanette Corder, wrote offering to play the part of Queen Victoria and was willing to 'come all the way from Nashville, Tennessee'. She wrote to the Pageant authorities:

I wonder of you have found the person who answers the qualification for the Queen. If not, I might be able to fit the bill. I am normally 20^1/2 inches around the waist, but I can easily be drawn in to eighteen inches and no doubt wear the dress required. I am 5ft 4 inches tall, weigh 110lbs and have blonde hair and blue eyes. I have definite dramatic ability and have made considerable progress as a singer, appearing on Radio programmes and on the stage. [6]

The scenario for these first seven episodes was devised by S C Kaines Smith, but the final episode was the work of Mr H Gordon Toy, who had worked previously with Gwen Lally in Warwick and had been appointed as chief stage manager. This was:

Episode 8. Modern and Industrial Birmingham which included a cavalcade of famous citizens, in some cases played by their descendants, followed by floats representing the different industries of Birmingham, parades from various organisations including; Boy Scouts, Girl Guides, British Red Cross Society, St John Ambulance Brigade, Disabled Ex-Servicemen's Association and the armed forces. There was then a floodlight 'Jewel Ballet' in which girls from the Jewellery quarter performed a dance in which they represented the different gems used in the trade. After this the floats and all performers assembled to form a gigantic 'Hub of Industrial England' which rotated slowly around the arena.

Throughout the 'Episodes', incidental music was played by an orchestra of forty with city organist G D Cunningham acting as grand master of music and Harold Gray as assistant. This included the theme from the film *Things to Come*, *Mars* from Holst's *Planets Suite* and incidental music to Purcell's *King Arthur*, which must have been much needed, as the Pageant performance was entirely non-speaking.

On 25 March the pageant workshops in Cambridge street were formally opened by the Lady Mayoress and from then until the start of dress rehearsals, at the beginning of July, they were a hive of activity under the direction of Miss Jean Campbell, mistress of the robes, and Bernard Coaling the pageant property master. More than 6,000 costumes and 12,000 properties were assembled not least of which were Egbert, Ogbert and little Sidney, the dinosaurs who made such a memorable contribution to the prologue. In fact for many people, who have seen the newsreels and other film that survives from the occasion, they are the enduring image of the Pageant itself. These monsters were constructed from huge quantities of plywood and canvas, with the largest being sixty feet long and standing nearly twenty feet tall. They were supported on an internal trolley propelled by two men with another four men working the legs while a seventh sat on the trolley to work the gadgets, which enabled the creature to roar and emit smoke. There seems to have been some confusion with dragons in this, but it comes as some relief to read that they were intentionally comic and Gwen Lally even suggested that they might 'enlist the services of George Robey as a prehistoric man'. Unfortunately he must have been busy at the time as this came to nothing.

Six hundred suits of armour, ten thousand arrows, five hundred bows, seven hundred swords and five hundred lances were amongst the many weapons assembled in the workshops. This production line was even inspected by the Minister for War, Mr Hore-Belisha, during his visit to Birmingham for the Territorial recruiting campaign. Hopefully he was not looking for any tips for rearming the country.

A 'crow's nest' was constructed high above Aston Park where Gwen Lally was able to sit with a clear view of the whole arena, and a battery of microphones, switches and loudspeakers enabled her to communicate with, and direct her troops below.

She was regarded as something of a 'character' by her recruits and was not averse to employing a few tricks to assert her superhuman dominance over the proceedings. It has been said, for example, that she would shout to a group of men a huge distance away 'you over there, why are you wearing a watch?' when she could not possibly see, relying on the fact that some recalcitrant would indeed be wearing one.

As well as decorations throughout the city centre, particularly in New Street and Corporation Street, two statues were erected at either end of Broad Street at two of the City's principal landmarks, Five Ways and the Hall of Memory. These twelve feet nude figures, of a man standing astride a model of Birmingham's civic buildings, were decorated in green and gold and were the work of Mr W Haywood, a Birmingham architect, who was consultant to the Decorations sub committee of the City Council. In a now rather familiar scenario there followed protests in the press claiming that they were improper and causing embarrassment to women in nearby offices. This led the Birmingham sculptor, Mr William Bloye ARBS, to leap to their defence stating:

> *the figures are symbolic and only interpretations of the human figure, with certain made up proportions to give them a heroic aspect.*[7]

Right up until the week before the opening appeals where still being made for volunteers to come forward and some scenes were not rehearsed until four days before the first performance on 11 July.

However, despite the potential for disaster, this performance went without any major hitches, although it is certain there were plenty behind the scenes. It was well received by the press the Birmingham Mail called it 'a veritable triumph of determination and enthusiasm over pessimism, difficulties and detraction.'

The *Post* described it as 'the finest spectacle that Birmingham has ever seen: it is a triumph of organisation in massed assembly.'

The *Gazette* although generally enthusiastic did make a few comments regarding its length,

> *magnificent in fact inspiring though it is as a spectacle, industrial Birmingham, which has to rise early for work, does not want to be kept at Aston Park until well after 11 o'clock.*

The Battle of Crecy, which proved to be one of the highlights of the show, became progressively more enthusiastic throughout the week, with at least fifty performers finding themselves with minor injuries in the hospital tents. This led to St John Ambulance men being disguised as the dead and dying on the field so that they could make hasty interventions when required. (Figure 5)

The Royal visit was planned for the matinee performance on 14 July but due to illness the King and Queen were not able to attend so their place was taken by the Duke and Duchess of Gloucester who received 'a really affectionate welcome'. *The Times* continues to describe their visit,

> *of the many scenes of loyal enthusiasm which have been crowded into this day none is more memorable than the tumultuous cheering of the great concourse of people who filled every available space in Victoria*

Figure 5. The Battle of Crécy. *Birmingham Reference Library.*

square, at the heart of the city, as the Royal visitors drove up to the council house. That was early in the afternoon, before they took luncheon with the Lord Mayor and other prominent citizens. But again late in the afternoon the royal car passed that way on the final stage of this visit, and the crowds seemed as big as ever and were no less enthusiastic. The principal event in this Royal visit has been the opening of the Birmingham Hospitals Centre, an enterprise unique in this country and a happy augury for Birmingham's second century of civic life. The presence of the Prime Minister, accompanied by Mrs Chamberlain, in the Royal party today has been a pleasant reminder of his family's proud record in the history of this progressive city and

Figure 6. The Parade near Aston Hall. Note the specially constructed 'Priestley House' that was burnt down a storey at a time on consecutive nights. *Birmingham Reference Library.*

in the statesmanship of the nation.[8]

The final part of their visit was to Aston Park (Figure 6) where they met the Pageant organisers and watched about an hour of the performance. After they left, their vacated box was taken over by members of the Australian cricket team, who were playing at Edgbaston that week. They may have witnessed the following:

> **Dead, 'But they wouldn't lie Down'** *There was an unrehearsed incident yesterday in the Birmingham Centenary Pageant, soon after the Duke and Duchess of Gloucester had left. In the Battle of Crecy scene a horse and cart were being used to carry 'the dead' from the field of battle when the horse bolted. Two 'dead men' who were in the cart got up and jumped out, while the horse raced on to crash into some railings at the side of the arena. No one was injured.*[9]

The Pageant was planned to be performed every evening between 11 and 16 July with two matinees, but its run was extended for an extra week partly due to demand but also due to the fact that bad weather had adversely affected ticket sales.

The Pageant certainly achieved its aim in being spectacular centenary celebration, and it gained a tremendous amount of publicity at home and abroad for Birmingham itself. Many children were taken to seethe performance, but on talking to them now it seems that over sixty years later they only have the vaguest memories of what actually went on. For local people it was the sight of the performers arriving at the park in costume that has provided the most lasting memory. In some publicity photographs knights in armour are even shown riding bicycles. Changing must have been a problem as some women evidently preferred to travel on the tram wearing their crinolines, but in order to assist mobility only inserted their 'hoops' when they arrived at the grounds.

For the performers themselves this was a wonderful opportunity to experience something different and exciting, to learn new skills and to make new, and in many cases, lasting friends. A number of pageant clubs where formed and Gwen Lally confidently predicted 'several weddings to result'.

It was not until February 1939 however that the true financial implications of the Pageant were revealed. A report from the General Purposes Committee showed that the total cost of production had been £31,735 and the income £17,900 giving an adverse balance of £13,835. Even when the Lord Mayor's contingency money was set against this there was a loss of £11,835. This prompted a heated debate in the press, and in a Council meeting where Mr Dennis Heath remarked on the charge of £1,600 for the horses 'there must have been Derby winners among them' and on the charge of £1,261 for music 'the rate must have been about £1 per bar'.[10]

On seeing these figures Gwen Lally wrote to both the *Mail* and the *Post* saying:

> *Sir I have only just seen the statement of expenses for the Birmingham Pageant. Much to my surprise, I read that the list started with 'the Pageant Master's fee -£850'. In fairness to myself, may I explain that my contract was for £600 production fee, the extra £50 being for the last 3 days of the extended week of the Pageant, the first three days of which I gave my services gratis. The remaining sum of £200 was for my expenses, which included living, travelling, secretary's salary and running expenses of a car. When such a sum as £850 is published as my fee, it is not only misleading, but a misrepresentation of facts.*[11]

These sums of money although of little consequence today were not inconsiderable at the time, and it is not really surprising that there was some grumbling, but set against this was the tremendous achievement of co-ordinating and producing a spectacle on such a grand scale, and seen by so many people, with the involvement of some twelve thousand volunteers. A task which would surely be impossible today. Also it should be remembered that The Pageant perhaps represented a last chance for innocent celebration and enjoyment, which contrasted starkly with events in Europe which would lead to the outbreak of war little more than twelve months later.

Notes and References

1. Pageant of Birmingham, *Birmingham Gazette*, Supplement, 1938.
2. *Birmingham Mail*, 21.1.1938.
3. *Birmingham Post*, 17. 2 .1938.
4. *Birmingham Gazette*, 4.4.1938.
5. *Birmingham Mail*, 29.6.1938.
6. *Evening Despatch*, 6.7.1938.
7. *Evening Despatch*, 12.7.1938.
8. *The Times*, 15.7.1938.
9. The *Northern Echo*, 13.7.1938.
10. *Evening Despatch*, 7.2.1939.
11. *Birmingham Mail*, 22.2.1939.

4. Birmingham and the Spanish Civil War

by Peter Drake

THE SPANISH CIVIL WAR, which began in July 1936 and ended with Franco's victory in April 1939, evoked strong emotions all over Europe. Spain was the precursor to the conflict which was to engulf the world a few months after the final defeat of the Spanish Republicans. Much has been written and documented about Birmingham's suffering and contribution to the Second World War but the city's reaction to the Spanish conflict throws an interesting sidelight on politics and public opinion in the city in the years of uneasy peace before 1939. This essay aims to shed some light on a time when 'Spain' meant more to Brummies than sea, sand and sangria.

Open virtually any Birmingham newspaper in the nearly three years the Spanish Civil War lasted and you cannot but be struck by the amount of coverage given to the war. The respective fortunes of the Spanish Republicans and the rebel Army forces led by General Franco were continually front page news. Apart from the obvious interest in a horrific conflict being enacted so close to our shores the wider implications of Spain were not lost on public opinion in this country. The battle between Spanish Nationalists backed by Fascist Italy and Germany and the left-wing democratically elected Republican Government of Spain seemed to prophesy the wider attack on the Western democracies which broke out in 1939. The aerial bombardment of Spanish towns by Franco's airforce and Italian and German planes which was such a feature of the civil war woke the citizens of British cities to the risks that those planes could be turned on them. This was, of course, all the more worrying to a city like Birmingham with its 'shadow' factories turning out armaments for the country's defence. There was also the humanitarian aspect to the Spanish conflict with Birmingham heavily involved in aiding the victims of the war especially children. The war had an appreciable effect, as well, on the political life of the city particularly on the parties on the Left, the local Labour and Communist parties. Finally there is the question which is always asked about British involvement in the Spanish Civil War – about how many Birmingham men went to fight in Spain. Who were they and what is the legacy of their actions?

In the interwar period Brummies had a choice of two local morning newspapers, the *Birmingham Post* and the *Birmingham Gazette*, the latter then coming up to 200 years of production, and two evening papers, the *Birmingham Mail* and the *Evening Despatch*. Before television public the opinion-makers were the press and newsreels and the influence of regional papers was certainly greater than today. So how did the Birmingham papers report the Spanish war?

It was undoubtedly well documented given the amount of space which reflected the war's international significance. Apart from the news pages all the Birmingham newspapers carried numerous editorials about the war as well as background articles and lively letter pages. What attitudes did the papers take?

In broad terms, despite some differing political stances, they more or less took the same line. This can be summarised as,

> *atrocities on both sides, Britain right not to be involved and the Non-Intervention Agreement should be supported.*

There was a marked hardening in the papers' attitude to Franco after the bombing of the Basque town of Guernica by German aircraft on 26 April 1937, the most infamous of all of the atrocities of the war. The flagrant violations of the Non-Intervention Agreement by Franco's allies, Hitler and Mussolini, were a major factor behind swinging British public opinion to the Republican side. In the 1930s Birmingham also possessed a weekly left-wing newspaper, the *Town Crier*. This was a four page broad sheet produced for the Labour Movement with a tiny circulation barely reaching two thousand.

However as a paper of record chronicling the activities which went on in Birmingham in support of the Spanish Republican cause it is brilliant. Every week it carried notices of forthcoming rallies and demonstrations for Spain, reports on previous week's activities, details of the various Aid for Spain Funds and lists of contributors, information on Birmingham Volunteers for Spain and correspondence and articles illuminating all the domestic political issues which were triggered off by the events in Spain. (Figure 1)

Having looked at the shaping of local opinion by the press it is now

Figure 1. A pamphlet printed in Birmingham in support of the Popular Front. *Birmingham Reference Library.*

time to examine more closely how the city was affected by the Spanish Civil War. At the outset it is important from a historical perspective to keep the reaction in perspective. The war did dominate the press and there were rallies and demonstrations on a scale that has never taken place again but it was largely within a political framework and, even then, there were complaints of indifference from activists. This is tellingly illustrated by a lament made by Hubert Humphreys, a Birmingham Labour councillor who went on a British fact-finding mission to Spain in early 1938. Shortly after his return he is quoted as saying:

> *I feel just as serious now as I did in Madrid over the situation, but I am at a loss what to do next. I keep on talking to meetings and groups but it was not exactly inspiring to find only fifty people in Birmingham sufficiently interested to turn up to my meeting for first hand information.*

On the other hand for activists and that really means supporters of the Spanish Government these were invigorating days when the future of democracy appeared to being decided on the Spanish mainland. As one activist put it to me:

> *We thought it was an exciting time to be alive. We were always out doing something whether collecting for Spanish children, chalking on the pavement advertising meetings or distributing literature.*

Birmingham held numerous rallies in support of Spanish democracy, ranging in size from major meetings at the Town Hall with national speakers like Clement Attlee and Aneurin Bevan to factory gate demonstrations usually addressed by local Communists. Surprisingly at a time when Oswald Mosley's Blackshirts were still active in the city there was never any reported public disturbances at any of these demonstrations, although many activists were convinced, and I am sure rightly convinced, that Special Branch informers were present at many of them. This was particularly likely to be the case because of the prominent Communist Party participation in the agitation and because of the fears of the authorities that these meetings were used as recruiting points for attracting Volunteers for Spain, which was illegal after the first few months of the war.

There were no public meetings supporting Franco at all.

A little bit needs to be said now about the organisation of the Spanish agitation in Birmingham. Remarkably much of the impetus behind all of the activity came from one woman, Mrs A M Newth.

Figure 2. A leaflet in support of the Popular Front. *Birmingham Reference Library.*

She was a relative newcomer to Birmingham at the outbreak of the Spanish War, having taken up a teaching appointment at King Edward's School while her husband lectured at Birmingham University. At the time her politics were on the fringe of being communist but she worked unstintingly with all persuasions. In 1935 she had organised the formation of a new pressure group in the city called the Birmingham Council for Peace and Liberty. The original motivation behind it had been a civil liberties one, protesting at police interference with trade union recruitment. Just prior to the outbreak of the conflict in Spain the Council was active in the defence of two men arrested for distributing trade union literature outside factories in the city. The two men, Bert Williams and John Cornford, were to be very significant in the reaction to Spain in Birmingham. Williams was the Midlands organiser of the Birmingham Communist Party who was to go to Spain with the International Brigades. His colleague on this occasion was a young Cambridge poet who was temporarily in Birmingham for personal reasons and who was one of the first to volunteer for Spain and one of the first to be killed. (Figure 2)

The Birmingham Council for Peace and Liberty organised a 'John Cornford lorry' which was sent to Spain to help with the evacuation of civilians from Madrid early in 1937. As well the Council organised Spain Weeks, commissioned another lecturer at Birmingham University, Helen Grant, to write a pamphlet about the background to the war, ran a Spain shop on Corporation Street and generally co-ordinated all the pro-Spanish agitation in the city. Mrs Newth, who I interviewed many years later, was also an indefatigable letter writer on behalf of the Spanish cause to the local press. How was it, therefore that such a recently formed body as the Council could have such an influence? The main reason was a political one. Reaction to the Spanish Civil War on the Left in British political circles was not as straightforward as most subsequent accounts have suggested. The usual view is that the war galvanised the Left including the Labour Party and pointed the way to the revived party which was to sweep to victory in the 1945 General Election. However this hides the difficulties the Spanish War raised for the Labour Party both locally and nationally. In particular, the issue of the Labour Party's relationship with the Communist Party was central to the domestic response to Spain. Calls for a United Front linking the parties of the Left and later, as opposition to the appeasement policies of the Chamberlain Government increased after the Munich Agreement, for a Popular Front including Liberals and Conservative opponents of Chamberlain, were highly popular with activists within local Labour Parties but not at all popular with the national leadership. In Birmingham it was politically expedient for both the local Labour and Communist Parties to allow the Birmingham Council for Peace and Liberty to set the agenda for the Spanish agitation, allowing Communists and Labour Party members to work together.

It has to be said as well that the other reason why the Council was such a galvanising body was to do with its leaders. Mrs Newth and her friends from the world of the University and other professions brought an administrative drive and competence and flair for publicity which the established labour movement had hitherto lacked. Spain became the raison d'être of the Council and it was no coincidence that once the war had ended in defeat the Council faded from sight.

The two remaining aspects of the reaction to Spain in Birmingham are the humanitarian response and the question of Birmingham men who went to fight in Spain. The humanitarian aspects have already been touched on in print in a book by Jim Fryth entitled *The Signal Was Spain: The Aid Spain Movement in Britain* (London, 1986) and in an article in the *Birmingham Historian* (number 14) on Basque children in the Midlands. It is worth emphasising though the extent of the relief work which went on in the city. Reports of the totals raised for Spanish relief appeared in the *Town Crier* every week and included donations from every section of the Labour Movement, from ward and constituency Labour Parties, from trade union branches, from the League of Youth, from Co-operative Women's Guilds and from the Fabian Society in Birmingham. There was a Milk for Spain campaign, collections for a Spanish foodship, for the Spanish Medical Aid Committee and for the International Brigades Dependants Aid Committee. Special efforts were made for the Basque children displaced in Franco's advance on their homelands leading to the establishment of a Birmingham Lord Mayor's Spanish Refugee Children's Relief Fund. Jim Fryth in the book quoted above has termed the Aid for Spain movement 'the most outstanding example of international solidarity in British history' and Birmingham was in the forefront of this activity.

Finally the most discussed aspect of British involvement in the Spanish Civil War is the International Brigades. Birmingham, along with nearly every part of this country, sent its volunteers to fight on behalf of the Spanish Government with altogether over two thousand British men leaving these shores. The largest contingent of British volunteers went to fight alongside their colleagues from around the world as part of the Communist controlled International Brigades. In Birmingham the arrangements for sending volunteers were operated by the local Communist Party and were the responsibility of the two full-time officials Jim Crump, Birmingham organiser, and Bert Williams. There was an unofficial quota which the national leadership wanted local areas to achieve. However recruiting and indeed enlisting was illegal so that the Party did not really recruit, rather it selected volunteers from those mainly Party members who wanted to go out and facilitated the arrangements. There is a very readable account of the one Birmingham volunteer to record his experiences in print. This is *Toolmaking and Politics: The Life of Ted Smallbone* (Compiled by Howard Williamson, Birmingham,1987). Jim Crump was in charge of the selection of volunteers and not everybody who volunteered was sent. Interviewing him many years later he told me that he had to be sure of men's motives, weeding out the possible police spies. Ideally volunteers were members of the Communist Party already, did not have young families and perhaps had had some military experience. After vetting by Crump the volunteers were sent on to London to catch the boat train to Paris and then on to Spain.

The Birmingham Communist leadership did have difficulties in meeting their quota. There were several reasons for this but all were related to the weakness of the broader Labour Movement in Birmingham in the interwar period. The local Communist Party itself was numerically small, the Labour Party in Birmingham seemed to be in perpetual opposition without a single MP and the trade unions fragmented to the point where the city's Public Relations Department appealed for employers to move to Birmingham because of the low wages paid here. Whereas other large industrial areas had a history of working class militancy based on single industries and a coherent trade union movement Birmingham presented a different challenge and indeed the aphorism

'Birmingham is different' was always being quoted on the Left. This underlying weakness in the Labour movement was reflected in the numbers of volunteers for Spain A much more cohesive area, but not larger in terms of population, like the South Wales valleys, saw nearly two hundred men depart for Spain. Proportionally with a population a fiftieth of the whole country Birmingham might have been expected to have sent fifty or so men whereas less than twenty actually went. At this distance of time it is not possible to be completely precise with numbers so one or two men could have gone and not been recorded in contemporary newspaper accounts or in the records of the British Battalions of the International Brigades. Also there is an element of imprecision about what constitutes a volunteer from Birmingham. This is highlighted by the fact that Birmingham was seeing workers arriving in the city throughout the 1930s from other more depressed areas of the country. Recognising these difficulties I have settled upon a figure of sixteen for the Birmingham volunteers, not a large number perhaps, but each one the product of an idealistic desire to defeat Fascism in another country and to sacrifice their lives for that cause.

Some of the information on the volunteers below is very vague and certainly does not do justice to the personal histories of this unique group of men but it is the best that can now be compiled. The two main sources of names and biographical information are an article in the *Birmingham Gazette* of 14 December 1938 and the lists of British volunteers compiled by the International Brigades Association. The one general point I would like to emphasise from my researches into the Birmingham volunteers is that none of them fit into the categories often designated for the volunteers, that is unemployed, escaping personal problems and probably poets. This list can never be definitive but I hope it, in some way, rescues from obscurity, a number of brave and idealistic Birmingham men.

The Birmingham Volunteers for Spain
Victor Barr
Born 1916. An Irish Catholic from Belfast. Left Ireland in 1934 and came to live in Birmingham with his brother Billy. Imprisoned in St Pedro jail with Bert Fletcher. Repatriated February 1939. Returned to his Birmingham address but was subsequently deported to Eire in the wake of IRA outrages. Evidence of his 'dangerous' political views on the Irish situation appeared to be his time in Spain. Joined the British Army in Belfast but, on a subsequent visit to Birmingham was arrested and deported for breaking his deportation order.

George Battle
Seriously wounded in Spain. Reported to be still in hospital in Spain in December 1938. No other information.

Edwin Bee
A native of Stafford, he was in his early thirties when he volunteered. He had worked as a draughtsman in Birmingham for five years before volunteering. Served as a cartographer with the XVth Brigade. Returned from Spain, December 1938.

Dr Colin Bradsworth
Aged forty-one when he volunteered. A General Practitioner with a surgery in High Street, Saltley. A native of West Bromwich, he was educated at Birmingham's premier school, King Edward's, New Street, and at Birmingham University. Served as a probationary surgeon in the Mediterranean during the Great War. After some years at the Queen's Hospital in Birmingham he set up his Saltley practice in 1927. A bachelor, he was active in Labour circles for many years and stood as the Independent Labour Party candidate for Rotton Park Ward in 1933. Joined the Communist Party in 1935. Volunteered for service with the British Medical Unit in October 1936 but when he reached London he found he was not needed and returned to Birmingham. Finally left in December 1936. Served as a medical officer, losing a thumb. Founded the Clarion Singers on his return to Birmingham in May 1938 to popularise Spanish Republican songs. Kept up his interest in the Clarion Singers and the International Brigade Association until his death in a road accident in 1958.

Tom Bromley
Living in Smethwick with his parents at the time he volunteered. Single in his early twenties. Employed at Midlands Counties Dairies in Birmingham as a bottler. He was a very intense young man whom his work colleagues failed to persuade not to go to Spain. A Communist sympathiser but probably not a party member. Killed at Gadesa on 3 April 1938.

Bert Fletcher
A married man living with his wife in Glebe Farm, Birmingham. A railwayman, a member of the National Union of Railwaymen and a dedicated Communist. Volunteered in January 1938. Imprisoned in St Pedro jail, Burgos, for ten months before being repatriated in

February 1939. Returned to Birmingham in very poor health. Later became the District Secretary of the International Brigade Association and a regular Communist candidate at local elections. He was killed in a railway shunting accident in 1964.

Oliver Green

A Birmingham printer and Communist. When he volunteered early in 1937 Jim Crump phoned the Communist Party National offices in King Street to get permission for him to go. While in Spain Green was one of the compilers of *La Livre de la 15eme Brigade Internationale*.

Harry Grocock

Aged twenty-five when he volunteered and living in Tenby Road, Moseley. A painter and decorator by trade working for Birmingham Corporation. Delegate to the Birmingham Trades Council from the National Society of Painters. Secretary of the International Peace Council and a Communist Party member. Went out to Spain early in 1938 and was imprisoned in Burgos. Returned to Birmingham in November 1938. Killed during the Second World War.

Jack Kremner

Of Jewish extraction from Manchester, he came to Birmingham shortly before volunteering. He was living in Erdington while working as a self-employed trader. In his late twenties when he went out to Spain where he saw service in transport. Returned to Birmingham in December 1938 but soon left for London.

Arthur McNally

A teenager originally from Durham but then living in Kings Norton. A builder's labourer and a member of the Young Communist League. His father was active in Labour circles and served on the Northfield Spain Aid Committee. Volunteered in January 1938 and was killed two months later on the Aragon front.

Clement Nicholas

A young commercial traveller from Handsworth. Not a Communist, he went out in Spring 1937 mainly serving on the Ebro front. Returned to Birmingham, without injury, with the main contingent of British volunteers in December 1938.

Thomas Simmons

A building labourer and veteran of the Great War. Lived at Tavistock Road, Hall Green.

Ted Smallbone

A twenty-nine year old single man living at his family home in Cotteridge. Had worked at Cadburys since 1924, mainly as a night shift worker on the wrapping machines. He had travelled abroad on Cadbury sponsored trips including two weeks in Geneva studying the League of Nations. Joined the Labour Party in the late twenties and then left for the Communist Party in 1931. Was dismissed from Cadburys in 1937 for his political activities and volunteered for Spain soon after. Saw front line action on the Ebro where he was wounded. Afterwards returned to Birmingham as a toolmaker, a shop steward and a Communist.

William Taylor

A transport driver employed by the BSA in Birmingham. Living at his family home in Small Heath. In his thirties he had fought in the trenches in the Great War. A Labour Party voter deeply affected by the Fascist atrocities in Spain. Worked in transport in Spain, serving for nearly two years.

Bernard Taylor

A twenty-seven year old lorry driver from Lodge Road Hockley. Became interested in politics shortly before volunteering as a result of attending a Spain demonstration in the city. Joined the Communist Party and went out at the beginning of 1937. Was captured at Jarama and repatriated in May 1937. The first volunteer to return to Birmingham. He addressed several meetings in the Birmingham area before going back to Spain in August 1937. He served for another year before going to work for the Communist Party in London.

Bert Williams

A forty-two year old married man with one child living in Olton. An ex-miner from South Wales, former secretary of the Porthcawl Labour Party and subsequently a dedicated Communist. Midland organiser of the Communist Party and regarded as a theoretician. Went out in February 1937 serving as Political Commissar for the British Battalion. Repatriated in August 1937 to continue his party work in the Midlands.

5. THE CHILDREN'S EMIGRATION HOMES

by Valerie Hart

THE CHILDREN'S EMIGRATION HOMES were founded in 1872 by Sir John Middlemore, a member of the notable Birmingham family. This is how he later described the incident which started it all off:

> *One day early in the year 1872 I was stopped near my father's house in St James' Road by a ragged little urchin who asked me to give him a copper. I told him I could do something better than that for him. I believed I could get him to Canada and give him a start in life there.*[1]

On impulse he took the lad with him, collected a number of other ragged little boys he found begging in New Street, and took them all home with him, 'greatly to the horror of the servants'. He was struck with the idea of rescuing these children from their desperate living conditions and offering them a new life by enabling them to emigrate.

An impulsive gesture this may have been and certainly John Middlemore himself identified this episode as the origin of his great scheme, but it was not ill informed. At this time John Middlemore was twenty-eight years old, recently returned from a four year stay with cousins in America, during which period he had achieved a degree in medicine and travelled widely through the mid-west and Canada. He had strongly held religious views and was actively seeking a cause to which he could commit himself.

In Birmingham there were two orphanages and the workhouses, but the streets were full of homeless and destitute children, as indeed were the streets of London and other large towns. Lord Shaftesbury estimated in 1847 that there were over 30,000

> *naked filthy, roaming and lawless children in London alone. Many slept at night under dry areas of bridges and viaducts, under porticoes, sheds and carts, in outhouses, in sawpits, on staircases and in the open air.*[2]

Thousands never obtained a meal except by begging and stealing. His network of Ragged Schools was an attempt to provide something better for these children and he organised the emigration of small numbers of them to both Canada and Australia.

Then, in 1869, a remarkable woman Maria Rye, impressed by the work of Lord Shaftesbury and her own experience of assisting families to emigrate, wrote a letter to *The Times* headed 'Our gutter children'. In this she argued that a new life abroad was the best opportunity for these children.

> *What treatment will they receive in our gutters; what justice will they receive from our hands when the police, the gaol and the hospital receive them? Can anything I introduce them to in Canada be worse than that to which they are doomed if we leave them where they are now?*[3]

In October 1869 she set sail for Canada with seventy-five girls between the ages of four and twelve, taken from workhouses. This was the start of a huge wave of child emigration.

Meanwhile another woman, Annie Macpherson, was independently organising a similar scheme for poor children from the East End of London, arriving in Canada the following year with a party of 100 young boys.Both women had observed at first hand in America that children orphaned by the Civil War could be fostered out to rural farming families.

John Middlemore was undoubtedly influenced by these remarkable new initiatives. The original name of his scheme was *The Gutter Children's Homes* and the first Annual Report describes in graphic terms the children he was trying to help:

> *No one who has a visitor's acquaintance with the lowest districts of Birmingham or other of our large English towns, can fail to report that a multitude of children are not only born and bred in crime, but that, from a mere coercion of circumstances they have little other than the idle, vagrant and criminal life open to them. Thus they become lawbreakers and outcasts from all human regard and a source of ruin and degradation to others.*

His aims were clear: 'To assist and save those children who are beyond the reach of our existing Government institutions'. The children he was targeting were those actively at risk of embarking on a criminal life, and emigration was seen as a way of permanently separating them from their old associations. In his own words:

> *Birmingham is the worst place for the child of a Birmingham criminal. Let them be taken right away – be seasick, see icebergs, learn to talk though their noses of dollars and cents, and have their lives turned entirely upside down. The New World is, in the fullest sense of the word, a new world to them.*

Snatched from an urban existence, the children were to be

transplanted to the backwoods of Canada, the younger children to be adopted by childless couples and the older ones to be employed as domestic servants or farm labourers.

> *Emigration is necessary to ensure the permanence and completeness of our children's reformation. As we rescue them more from their bad associations than from their own vice, our work would be wholly incomplete if we settled them at last in Birmingham.*

He quickly set about the task of establishing his scheme. By June 1872 he had hired a house in St Luke's Road, Highgate, for boys and one in Spring Road, Edgbaston, for girls. These were to be residential reception homes for children collected from the streets. A place where they could be trained and prepared for emigration. He also started negotiations with the Canadian Agent.

In the first year, thirty-five 'gutter children' were taken in, and twenty-nine of these sailed with John Middlemore for Canada on board the *Sarmation* on 1 May 1873. On the same boat was a much larger contingent of seventy-five children accompanied by Maria Rye. The following year John Middlemore took fifty children and travelled on the same boat as Annie Macpherson and her party.[4]

This initial journey of John Middlemore's was surprisingly unplanned. He had gone to a great deal of trouble to establish his homes in England, to raise money, to train the children but yet no forward arrangements were made for their arrival. He describes this in the Annual Report.

> *The journey was entirely one of discovery and speculation. I had not a single friend in Canada and did not know what to do with my children when I arrived there. In the course of my enquiries I heard of the Hon. George Allan and Professor D. Wilson of Toronto, and sent them telegrams soliciting help. Both these gentlemen interfered most generously and cordially on my behalf. They procured temporary lodgings for my children and treated me with much personal kindness. My arrival was made known by articles in the Toronto newspapers and by correspondence and in the course of three or four weeks. I found good homes for all of my children.*

Obviously there was a need for a base in Canada and John Middlemore persuaded the City Council of London, Ontario, to provide a permanent Reception and Distributing House which opened in 1875 under the name *The Guthrie Home*. By 1879 new purpose built Homes were opened, too, in St Lukes Road, Birmingham with separate provision for both boys and girls. This was the fruit of long and ingenious fund raising.

John Middlemore himself devoted a lot of time to personal appeals for financial support. 186 donors and 130 subscribers are listed by name in the first Annual Report which was clearly fulfilling the need for accountability to funders. The list included many of Birmingham's most prominent families including Cadburys, Chamberlains, Kenricks, Joseph Gillott, Lord Calthorpe, Lloyds, Southalls, Tangyes, The Earl of Dudley, The Bishop of Worcester and a number of Middlemores. The account sheets for the first year to September 1873 shows an amazing charitable income of £2,537. Expenses included £2 2s 8d for 'pocket money and small presents for the children'.

Passage money to Quebec cost £142 19s 6d but rather charmingly this was 'minus cost of J T Middlemore's ticket, £31 10s'. The Ontario Government contributed £17 5s for the settlement of the children in Canada.

Churches of all denominations contributed to the cause, sometimes by contracting to pay for the support and settlement of one particular child. Door-to-door collections were often made, so we find, for example, that the inhabitants of St Lukes Road and Varna Road contributed £12 for the support of a boy called Henry Haynes in 1877. Gifts in kind were also welcome and the Annual Reports list an amazing array of these. For example 'twenty-two plum puddings', '6000 tracts' or 'white mice'. One Ladies Sewing Circle in 1877 donated the fruits of their labours: ninety-four night gowns, 102 pinafores, 105 chemises, seventy-eight petticoats, eighty hoods for Atlantic journeys and fifty-seven pillow cases. One lady, Mrs Bekenn, in 1876 gave 154 pairs of socks knitted by herself.

There were also fund raising events. An outstanding example was the grand Bazaar held in the Town Hall over five days in 1878. The various stalls were supplemented by a Japanese Village and Tea House with various other entertaining attractions. The total raised was £2000! (Figure 1).

John Middlemore's fund

Figure 1. Poster advertising Bazaar to raise funds for the Children's Emigration Homes. *V. Hart.*

raising success was phenomenal and undoubtedly due both to his persistent hard work and his dedication. He devoted his life to the cause, taking on the role of fundraiser, treasurer, collector of children, negotiator with the families and an active participant in the life of the Homes, as well as personally accompanying the children for many years to Canada and finding suitable places for them.

The Annual Reports give no indication of opposition to the principle of child emigration and present a glowing picture of success. However, there were strong criticisms of the child emigration schemes and it may be for this reason that the reports give considerable details about the desperate plight of the children they were taking to Canada.

Many of the children admitted to the Homes were orphans who had been forced on to the streets to beg a living. In the early days most came from the densely populated slum areas of central Birmingham, later cleared under Joseph Chamberlain's improvement schemes and replaced by Corporation Street.

Some of the children came from Balsall Heath. For example, one seven year old child 884 came from a widow in Jakeman's Walk. She said:

My husband has been dead two years. I go out washing and cleaning. I have had to sell most of my furniture to buy food and pay rent. Last week I sold my bedsteads..

The room contained nothing but a dirty mattress, some bedclothes, a candle and a lamp. She also had a twelve-month old baby in an emaciated condition.

One case in 1883 was that of a six-year old boy taken from a poor outcast woman living in Gullet Street. (Figure 2) The mother had been frequently in prison and was 'half intoxicated when I called for her little boy'. She was apparently eager for the child to go: 'Take him away from me, take him away from me' she said 'He has no chance with me.' The Annual Report of 1878 described a visit to a lodging house where there were thirteen children, four women and two men all living in one room, none of whom had any employment and therefore were solely dependent on begging or crime. It is difficult for us to imagine the desperate living conditions of many people before the introduction of the Welfare State.

Most of the children admitted to the homes were below thirteen years of age, and sometimes much younger than this. Poverty alone was not regarded as sufficient reason for a child's admission; there was usually some other contributory cause as well. Occasionally

Figure 2. 'The Gullet', Birmingham. *V. Hart.*

cases were recorded in the Annual Report, of poor women bringing children to the Homes and asking for them to be admitted, only to be turned away because their only problem was poverty.

The children spent varying amounts of time at the Homes, according to their dates of admission, since the emigrating party usually sailed to Canada in May each year. The intervening period was taken up with training them for their future lives. On admission to the Homes they were often disorganised, thriftless and lacking in social skills. They were taught cleanliness, obedience and healthy outdoor games, as well as being sent to the local schools regularly. This caused some difficulties for the schools involved since their stay was always temporary. They received pocket money and special prizes as well as punishments. Each year they had a Christmas tree and an annual picnic, but the emphasis was on a routine and well ordered existence. It sounds rather regimented but John Middlemore's comment in 1884 softens the picture somewhat:

Some may smile when we observe that we rely very much on the educational influence of games, pet rabbits and plots of garden for the children to call their own and that we often find attention to health and course of cod liver oil is more important to a boy or girl than the inculcation of the 3 Rs.

The Homes were run on a day to day basis by two matrons, one for the girls and one for the boys, with some assistance from a servant and cook. The 1881 Census gives a glimpse of the inhabitants. Ellen Evans was matron for the boys and was living there with her two daughters ages sixteen and seventeen, together with forty-eight boys of whom five were below five years of age, thirty-two were aged five to eleven and the remaining eleven were aged eleven to thirteen. It must have been a considerable task to look after them all. The girls' matron was Agnes Blackhall and she cared for twenty-three girls all of whom were in the age range two to nine years of age.

A consistent feature of all the institutions and child emigration homes was the splitting up of family groupings. The 'before and after' photographs of children at the Middlemore Homes shows brother and sisters together, but they were in fact separated on arrival and certainly allocated to separate families in Canada (Figure 3a, 3b, 3c).

At times there was some difficulty in managing the behaviour of large groups of children in the Homes, as indicated in the 1877 Annual Report when there were 105 children resident.

They had much to unlearn as well as to learn; deceit had been

Figure 3a. Thomas, Elsie May and Blanche R-, as they appeared when received into the Homes in November, 1908. *V. Hart.*

Figure 3b. Thomas, Elsie May and Blanche R-, as they appeared two months later in January 1909. *V. Hart.*

Figure 3c. Henry C- 1914... before and after. *V. Hart.*

Figure 4. Children's Emigration Homes, Birmingham. *V. Hart.*

familiar to them for many years, they were impatient under the restraints of the home, and they missed the excitement and freedom of their Arab life.

Most of the children stayed in the Homes less than a year. The 1886 Annual Report refers to a farewell meeting for parents and children on the eve of the departure for Canada. This must have been a sad occasion. There are also other references to family and friends coming to see them off. (Figure 4)

In 1879 on the 12 June we left New St Station for Liverpool with a

Figure 5. On the Ship. *V. Hart.*

party of ninety-one children, the great majority of whom were in boisterous spirits. A few tears may have been shed by some at parting from their friends who had assembled to see the last of them; but most were as radiant as health and hope could make them.

The journey itself must have been an amazing experience for the children. At Liverpool they embarked on a steamship for a voyage of thirteen days to Canada. The beginning of such a trip is described in the 1886 Annual Report:

We left Liverpool on 18 June. Our party consisted of 115 children - that is, seventy-eight boys and thirty-seven girls. As is usual, the more sensitive of the children showed by their subdued and clinging manner that they began their voyage with that sinking of heart - which doubtless comes from leaving all they care for at a time when they are tired and over-wrought, and which is in striking contrast to the buoyancy of spirit which they usually complete their voyage.

Almost immediately they struck bad weather and most of the children retired to bed for several days.

There was also the problem of the other passengers. In 1871 there were 600 other emigrants on board ship from all parts of Europe and 'all sorts and conditions of man'. In 1886 there was some concern to keep the boys away from association with the cattle drovers who were regarded as highly unsuitable. The children found ways to pass the time. (Figure 5)

As the voyage progressed the children amused themselves with swings which the sailors attached to booms, with skipping ropes, round games, with the old familiar Birmingham 'Stagalony' and one or two with reading'. Later in the journey they also encountered dense fog and drifting ice which delayed them for three days near the coast of Newfoundland.

Arrival in Quebec was by no means the end of the journey however. Next came an arduous journey of over 600 miles by train to London, Ontario. In 1879, this leg of the journey took from midday on 2 June to the evening of 24 July. The first night the ninety-one children slept on the train in exceedingly cramped conditions: two buckets of water were procured in which to sponge the children's hands and faces. Their caps were collected; the back of every alternate seat was reversed to as make a sort of sofa of the two adjoining seats, measuring four feet by two feet seven. On each of the sofas the children were arranged in parties of four or five. It was also dusty, hot and noisy. The party travelled by train without stopping till l am on 23 June when they disembarked to spend the night in 'the immigrant sheds' in Toronto, which don't sound very appealing! Finally, they reached Guthrie Home, the reception centre at London, Ontario (Figure 6).

The next step was for John Middlemore, often accompanied by someone else, to take off groups of children on settlement journeys to find suitable homes for them. Isolated backwoods areas were preferred since there was less temptation to run away. Younger children were chiefly placed for adoption with childless families. The older ones were to be employed but it was clear that they were always going to be a source of cheap labour.

> *A boy only ten years old can make himself of great use to a farmer in driving the cows to and from pasture or water, and in carrying drinking water for the refreshment of the farmer and his assistants when they are harvesting... A boy of twelve can harrow; a boy of*

Figure 6. Guthrie Home, the Reception centre in London, Ontario, 1888. *V. Hart.*

Figure 7. A party of girls about to start for Canada. *V. Hart.*

thirteen can cultivate; a boy of fourteen can plough.

For the child emigration movement as a whole it was the process of settling the children with families without adequate supervision, which attracted most criticism (Figure 7).

Various complaints were lodged which prompted the Local Government Board to commission one Andrew Doyle to conduct an investigation. He was particularly to enquire into the well-being of the workhouse children shipped out by Miss Rye and Miss Macpherson at the ratepayers' expense. He undertook the task very diligently and visited about 400 children as well as inspecting records and talking to officials. His report in 1875 was damning. He found 'intolerable evidence of ill-treatment, overwork and physical abuse' and raised serious questions about the proclaimed advantages of sending children abroad. The lack of follow-up inspection was a particular target of his criticism.[5]

The Middlemore Homes Annual Reports make no reference to this bombshell although it must have had considerable relevance.

Figure 8. John Middlemore with some Emigration Homes' Children. *V. Hart.*

The children settled in Canada by John Middlemore had very little ongoing support until the Guthrie Home opened in November 1875, some months later than the Doyle Report.

John Middlemore had instituted an Adoption Agreement, quoted in the first Annual Report:

I promise to take and adopt... and to treat him in all respects as if he were my own child; to attend to and supply all his needs; to send him to school and to church or chapel, and finally to teach him some trade or calling by attention to which he may make himself an honourable and independent person.

The difficulty with this was enforcement. It had no legal standing and even when inspection visits, were arranged in later years, they were necessarily brief and infrequent as the children were scattered geographically over such a wide and rural area. Doyle also collected some extraordinary statements from the children themselves. For example, one girl commented 'Doption, Sir, is when folks get a child with no wages.' (Figure 8)

It was probably in response to the Doyle Report however, that the Annual Report of 1876 gave full details of the 'safeguards for children'. These stated that each person applying for a child should be recommended that children should be visited when deemed necessary' and that the Middlemore Homes reserved the right to remove a child. Signed written agreements were required, which included a minimum wage clause requiring the families to pay between thirty-six and seventy-two dollars per year.

As the Guthrie Home became more established, farmers began to make applications in advance of the children's arrival, which was obviously a more suitable system. However, there seem to have been ongoing 'settlement journey' into outlying districts which are far from confidence-inspiring. One of these is described in the Annual Report of 1883. John Middlemore set off with a companion and fourteen children for Lucknow, which they reached by a train journey of about nine hours. They found many ready offers of homes immediately and child after child was left there. At last only one child remained. Mr Middlemore consulted a Mr Wilson whom he knew who lived in the back country. 'Our way lay along narrow lanes which had been cut through forest and swamp' They had a meal with Mr Wilson, who then offered to drive them to a family that would probably accept the child. As they set off again the child began to cry. 'Surely it was not hard to find the cause of his fears. Companion after companion had left him and I was about to leave him too.' After an hour's ride, they arrived at the farm only to find that the man of the house, a tall broad chested Scotsman, was working out in the fields, and his wife was reluctant to discuss the matter. In the end, the man willingly agreed but the wife sounds rather grudging. 'If you take the boy I will do my duty; if he does badly it won't be my fault',

Figure 9. Poster claiming 5,252 children taken to Canada, 1925. *V. Hart.*

The child was settled there, but occasionally offers of homes were refused if the people concerned did not display a sufficiently welcoming or Christian attitude.

The justification for the uprooting of these children was their eventual success in Canada, and the Annual Reports are full of stories about these. Most notable of them was the first boy ever to be admitted to the Homes, in 1872. At that time he had already been in prison in England three times. Yet, ten years later, he owned his own farm in Ontario and was doing well.

Some children's letters from Canada to Mr Middlemore are also quoted in the first Annual Report. One girl wrote: I have had good health since I came to Toronto, I have got fat and red cheeked now and I go to school every day.' Another boy finished his letter, 'I like Canada pretty well but I feel a little lonesome.'

One outstanding success story from the 1911 Report is worth a mention. Mr and Mrs Fred P were both ex-Middlemore Homes children. He was now Superintendent of a Sunday School in the district, which is where he met his wife. His former master sold him a farm on easy terms and Fred built his own homestead there. In 1911, the couple took a boy from the Home into their household.

There were, of course, some failures. Quite a large number of children each year returned to Guthrie House for resettling with a different family. A few ran away completely but on the whole it is surprising there weren't more of these, especially considering the enormous numbers of children involved. The 1894 report recorded an astonishing total of 2,215 children taken to Canada since the Homes started and by 1925, this number had risen to 5,252 (Figure 9).

Throughout the last part of the nineteenth century the tide of child emigrants from Britain continued to rise. John Middlemore consistently sent out an annual consignment, and occasionally more than this. For example in 1888 three groups of children were dispatched, totalling 249 children.

Figure 10. A new life in Canada. *V. Hart.*

Meanwhile, other organisations had entered the field including Dr Barnardos from 1882. Interestingly, his approach was considerably more ruthless than John Middlemore's. Barnardo believed strongly that the children's needs were paramount and that he could identify what they were. He declared in favour of the forcible removal of a child from unsuitable parents, a practice which he dubbed 'philanthropic abduction'.[6]

By the mid 1890s, the controversy over child emigration had increased. There was a noticeable change in Canadian attitudes and increasing anxiety about the type of child entering the country. Both the *Toronto News* and the *Toronto Globe* launched attacks on the system. 'Street waifs and inmates of reformatories, refuges and lodging houses are not the classes with which to build up a strong nationality.' The British were keen to ship out their problems and reduce the poor rates. Why should Canada oblige them?

One result of all this was an increasing prejudice against child immigrants which was fanned by widely publicised instances of criminal behaviour. In 1897 the Ontario legislature passed an *Act to Regulate Immigration* which instituted a proper inspection system for the children and various restrictions. Section 12 of the Act prohibited the immigration of any child, who has been reared or who has resided amongst habitual criminals', and also the children of confirmed paupers. Manitoba, Quebec and New Brunswick followed suit.

This was a major blow for the Middlemore Homes as well as other agencies and the numbers of children entering Canada dropped sharply. The Guthrie Home closed but was replaced by a new base called Fairview just outside Halifax, with increased emphasis on settlement of children in the maritime states.

New impetus was given to the whole movement by the shift in emphasis from the needs of the children to the needs of the Empire. Queen Victoria's Jubilee in 1897 marked a high point in Britain's imperial aspirations and emigration was seen as a means of strengthening imperial bonds. Even the Local Government Board succumbed to this persuasive argument and again allowed workhouse children to emigrate. After a brief pause during the First World War, the stream of children resumed, greatly encouraged by the *1922 Empire Settlement Act* which gave additional financial incentives for emigration to Canada. However, a well publicised series of tragedies involving cruelty to children finally led to yet more investigations and the Bondfreed Report of 1924, which at last imposed a ban on unaccompanied immigrants below the age of fourteen.

Coincidentally the autumn of 1924 also saw the death of John Middlemore. He had given his life to the work of child emigration. He was actively involved in the Homes for forty-two years and remained Hon Treasurer to his death. At first the future of emigration from the Middlemore Homes was uncertain but in fact the work continued in association with the Fairbridge Society, another emigration group which took children chiefly to Australia.

The original Homes in Highgate by now were no longer suitable and in 1929 new Homes opened in Selly Oak. These buildings were occupied until 1955 when the committee sold them to Birmingham City Council and they became Westhill College. Emigration ceased during the Second World War, but continued after the war until 1949. By now the *Children Act* of 1948 had changed the whole situation: Local authorities were to take the main responsibility for children needing protection. Since then the Middlemore Committee have diversified their work, developing support and residential centres for families in need.

Notes and References

1. 'I Remember', *Birmingham Gazette & Express*, 1907.
2. Hansard, 6 June 1848, quoted in *Children of the Empire*.
3. *The Times*, 29 March 1869.
4. Government of Canada Sessional Papers. Ship arrivals at the Port of Quebec.
5. *Children of the Empire*, Gillian Wagner.
6. Article in *Night and Day*, Vol LX.

Sources and Bibliography

1. Annual Reports of the Middlemore Homes.
Middlemore John, 'I Remember', *Birmingham Gazette & Express*, 1907. Ref: BRL 217750.
3. Census returns 1881.
4. *100 Years of Care*, published by the Middlemore Homes Committee.
5. *Lost Children of the Empire*, Bean & Melville.
6. *Children of the Empire*, Wagner Gillian.
7. Internet references: Government of Canada Sessional Papers. Ship arrivals at the Port of Quebec. www.ist.uwaterloo.ca/~marj/genealogy/ships/html.

6. Fit and Proper Councillors?

by Margaret Holmes

Representation on Birmingham Council 1838-1920

This meeting considers... a fit and proper person to represent the... ward on the Town Council.

E P HENNOCK QUOTES THE ABOVE words at the start of his book, words which have been used in support of candidates for election since 1835 when elections were first introduced into local government. He notes the ambiguity of these words and the fact that they raise more questions than they answer, asking to what ideas of fitness did men appeal when recruiting town councillors, and to what degree did the actual composition of any council reflect these ideas? Hennock is concerned with the relation between ideal and reality, specifically in the experience of the early Birmingham Council (and also Leeds, which is not relevant here).[1] He is not especially concerned with the extent to which councillors were representative in the sense that they reflected the communities from which they came. This aspect of local government has received more attention in recent decades, but in the nineteenth century it was more generally accepted that leadership should properly come from the 'responsible, educated classes of the community', what Burke called 'a natural aristocracy'. There was an unspoken assumption that this would consist of white middle or upper class males, an assumption which has been increasingly questioned in recent times.

The principle of elected local government in Britain was laid down by the *Municipal Corporations Act* of 1835, although Birmingham continued to be governed by Court Leet and Street Commission until 1838. Then, on the petition of the inhabitants, the Crown granted a municipal corporation on the model of the 1835 Act. A central feature of the system was the principle of unpaid service by citizens without special training. In 1948 payment for loss of earnings was introduced,[2] and at present councillors receive a minimal annual allowance plus a small attendance allowance, a limited amount of training is also available, but otherwise the basic principle still stands today, largely unmodified. Limited as the Council was in the nineteenth century in the degree to which it represented the population of the town as a whole, it tended to reflect those groups which were the most powerful.

Initially candidates for election to the Borough Council were restricted to ratepayers, as was the municipal electorate, but with the further qualification that they should pay rates of at least £30 or own property worth £1000. As late as 1861 candidates for election could have been no more than three per cent of the population, the size of the municipal electorate.

In 1869 women ratepayers were given the borough vote. They formed up to a fifth of the borough electorate, and by 1900 over a million women had the local government vote, although this was still only a fraction of the adult female population.[3] Women's right to sit on borough councils was not established until 1907, and in 1912 there were only two women on the Greater Birmingham Council. In 1882 the property qualification was virtually abolished, although in 1911 Birmingham's municipal electorate had only risen to nineteen per cent.[4] Given all these restrictions in the early years, Birmingham's first borough councillors were of necessity drawn from a very limited section of the population.

The first Town Council, which sat in 1839, consisted of sixty-four councillors. They were mainly small businessmen (fifty-five per cent), of whom thirty-six per cent were manufacturers, a small number of fairly large merchants, and a banker. About twenty per cent of the new councillors had previously been members of the Street Commission.[5] In the early years the Council was characterised by a preponderance of petty bourgeois representatives, whose main aim was to keep down the rates, a popular if short-sighted policy. Ratepayers associations were powerful pressure groups which had spokesmen on the Council in the 'Economist' group, notably Joseph Allday, the group leader. In 1855 they succeeded in vetoing a new Improvement Bill which was to have carried out a much needed programme of drainage, paving and street improvement, because of the necessary rate increase involved.[6] During this period the status of councillors was low. The local (largely radical non-conformist) elite of the town was active at this time, but looked to philanthropic rather than municipal outlets for their contributions of public service. By 1852 the big business section had grown a little to make up just over fifteen per cent of the membership, and the professions began to be represented, with three solicitors on the Council. In the late 1860s dramatic changes took place, due to an influx into the Council of several wealthy industrialists, the nonconformist elite who had previously eschewed

Council representation. By the late 1870s the small business group had been eclipsed by the number of big businessmen, which by then made up one quarter of the Council. This was the start of Birmingham's municipal reform movement, which was to lead the country in establishing the principle of state provision of the basic social amenities. An important contributing factor was the zeal of the radical non-conformists who preached. The 'civic gospel' as it was called. Radical preachers who expounded this 'gospel' urged believers to express their religious convictions in terms of civic duty, and in particular through the municipal corporation. Most prominent amongst the new entrepreneurial councillors was Joseph Chamberlain, a forceful and hard-headed businessman, who had transformed the fortunes of the family firm of screw manufacturers, Nettlefold and Chamberlain.[7] Chamberlain became mayor of Birmingham in 1873 and remained in this post until 1876. He was aided in his municipal ambitions by the Liberal 'caucus', which monopolised political representation in Birmingham during this period. At the heart of Chamberlain's civic renaissance lay the municipalisation of gas and water, in the implementation of which his skills as a shrewd businessman were invaluable. The whole programme of municipal reform which was carried out at this time came to be seen as a model for the rest of Britain, and even overseas.[8] It provided a new vision of the function of local government, and earned Birmingham the title of 'the best governed city in the world' according to R J Ralph in *Harper's Monthly* magazine, 1890.

In 1891 a boundary extension enlarged the size of the Council from sixty-four to seventy-two members. Big business continued to make up just over twenty per cent of the Council in the 1880s and 1890s, while the group of small businessmen contracted to fifteen per cent in 1896. In their discussion paper on businessmen on the Council Morris and Newton observe that some of the wealthiest family groups of businessmen on the Council towards the end of the nineteenth century were so closely inter-related and inter-married that they displayed, for many generations before the Second World War, many of the overlapping and interlocking characteristics which C Wright Mills claims for his power elite. They go on to say that this is a question which cannot be settled definitively, but certainly the family connections were extensive amongst a large number of wealthy businessmen who were highly active in the political life of the city and who appear to have been highly influential also. The biggest group involved the Chamberlains, Kenricks, Beales and Lloyds, all of whom were related by kinship ties as well as other interests.

Members of all these families were Mayors of Birmingham, as well as councillors. In the case of the Chamberlains and the Martineaus, family members were still on the Council in the 1960s. A second family tie-up of business Council members involves the Barrows and the Cadburys, who were related by marriage. Members of both families filled important positions on the Council, including Mayor. A member of the Cadbury family was a councillor until the 1960s and George Corbyn Barrow was Mayor in 1965, although by this time the influence of these groups of families on the Council was insignificant compared to former times. in those days they were also bound by powerful religious ties. The Chamberlains, Kenricks, Martineaus and the Nettlefolds were Unitarians, and the Cadburys, Lloyds and the Barrows were Quakers. Neither of these two dissenting religions were numerically significant in the city, but they had enormous influence over its political and social development. As Morris and Newton put it, these families met each other when they were working, playing and praying. Whether or not they could properly be classed as a power elite, they undoubtedly wielded an influence over the political affairs of the city which was quite disproportionate to their numbers.

Towards the end of the century the professional group grew steadily larger, until it was almost as large as the big business group in 1896. From the late 1870s up to 1911 the Council was dominated by a combination of big businessmen and professional men, especially doctors, although by 1902 the number of big businessmen had declined somewhat, to 16.7 per cent. The number of manual workers on the Council in 1882 was five. This period saw a more cautious approach to municipal change, compared to the dynamism of the 1870s. These were bad years for the metal and engineering industries, and Birmingham at the heart of the Black Country was feeling the decline in the area's coal, iron and steel industries. Thus a more cautious business ethos was developing, which fed directly into policy on the Council with its large business representation. It could be said that 'Backward' was more appropriate than the Council's motto 'Forward' particularly in the areas of municipal housing, transport, and electricity, where Birmingham was considerably behind other major cities. The two notable exceptions were the water supply, transformed by the Elan Valley project, and town planning; Birmingham had a considerable input into the influential *Housing and Town Planning Act* of 1909 under the influence of Neville Chamberlain, who chaired the Town Planning committee.

1911 marked the end of one era in Council history, for in that year Greater Birmingham was created. The Council in 1912 was not directly comparable to the preceding one having increased in size from seventy-two to 120. However, the percentage of big businessmen in 1912 remained much the same as in 1902 at 16.9 per cent although this was only fifteen councillors. This came as a disappointment to some of the advocates of the Greater Birmingham scheme, who had hoped that the inclusion of the new residential areas would bring more people of this kind into the Council and so re-establish the position that had existed in the 1880s and 1890s.[9] By contrast, the percentage of small businessmen rose from 16.7 per cent to 20.8 per cent, a return to a similar position as existed in 1876. But this change was entirely due to the city's new extended boundaries; in the old wards the proportion of small businessmen had remained the same, while in the new wards it was as high as 25.5 per cent. The percentage of professionals increased from eighteen per cent to 22.5 per cent, also the number of manual workers had risen slightly, from five to nine, 7.5 per cent of the total, linked to the fact that the Labour party was beginning to gain representation on the Council, with five councillors in 1911. The period from 1870 up to the First World War has been called the 'Golden Age of Local Government'. Since then, the occupational composition of town councils has changed considerably. However it is arguable that the lower profile and the reduced influence of local government is more attributable to a gradual diminution of its powers in favour of central government than to a reduction in the calibre of councillors.

Women on Birmingham Council

In Birmingham a strong women's movement grew up in the nineteenth century, and it was as an extension of this that women entered local government. Women were active in the Provincial School Boards and Birmingham was one of the first towns to have women Poor Law Guardians in the 1880s.[10] Standing for local government election involved the same notions of suffrage and service, philanthropy and practical Christianity and was therefore attractive to a certain section of middle-class women at that time. A campaigning group known as the Women's Local Government Society (WLGS) played an active part in obtaining the right for women to stand in local government Elections, and continued to support women seeking office. Women became eligible to stand on Parish and Rural District Councils in 1894,[11] and 1907 this was extended to all local authorities, including county councils and boroughs such as Birmingham. In 1911 two women joined the Birmingham Council, Mrs Ellen Hume Pinsent, nationally known for her work with the mentally handicapped, and Miss Marjorie Pugh. This brought the national total of women councillors to eighteen.[12] Due to the boundary extensions increasing the number of Birmingham wards from eighteen to thirty, both women stood in newly created seats. Mrs Pinsent stood as a Liberal Unionist, and Miss Pugh as an Independent Liberal. Miss Pugh was challenged by a Tory opponent who ran with the slogan 'Do you want to be represented by a businessman or a suffragette?' She beat him with the help of the women's movement and the WLGS. In 1913 Miss Clara Martineau was elected onto the Birmingham council, where she kept women's issues on the agenda.[13]

Notes and References

1. Hennock, E P, *Fit and Proper Persons, Ideal and Reality in Nineteenth Century Urban Government*, 1973, p1.
2. *Ibid.*, p4.
3. Hollis P, *Ladies Elect,Women in English Local Government 1865-1987*, p7.
4. Hennock, E P, *Fit and Persons*, p6.
5. *Ibid.*, p3.
6. *Ibid.*, p31.
7. D Judd, *Radical Joe, A Life of Joseph Chamberlain*, 1977, p18.
8. A Briggs, *History of Birmingham*, Vol 11, 1952, p67.
9. Hennock, E P, *Fit and Proper Persons*, p40.
10. Hollis P, *Ladies Elect – Women in English Local Government 1865-1964*, p239.
11. *Ibid.*, p9.
12. *Ibid.*, p397.
13. *Ibid.*, p458.

7. THE BIRMINGHAM MUNICIPAL BANK: A MUNICIPAL EXPERIMENT

by C J Brockie

A REDUNDANT BANK BUILDING stands at the bottom of Broad Street, opposite Birmingham's International Convention Centre. Its frontage is to be retained in the planned redevelopment of the site. This represents the last remnants of Britain's only Municipal Bank.

The First World War transformed Birmingham into the arsenal of the war effort. Major manufacturing companies like BSA at Small Heath, Kynoch's at Witton and Vickers-Metropolitan at Ward End, produced cartridges, shells, fuses, rifles, machine guns and aero-engines needed for the War.

Government borrowing increased to cover the escalating level of defence expenditure. The Chancellor of the Exchequer Reginald McKenna, introduced legislation to raise 'War Loans' in 1914 and 1915. A critic of the government's borrowing policy was the Lord Mayor of Birmingham, Neville Chamberlain. He wrote in November 1915:

> *I do not believe in McKenna's bonds... he is beginning at the wrong end... the real problem is to make a man save who hasn't saved before... . My idea generally is to start a municipal savings association. The town would guarantee the interest... to lend the scheme the prestige and weight of the local authority.*[1]

Government had considered raising small sums of money from the industrial workers. McKenna had invited larger Councils to form local Savings Committees. Birmingham, however, had no significant savings institutions, the City's last Trustee Savings Bank having closed in 1864.[2]

According to one account, the idea of establishing a Municipal Bank came to Chamberlain in a moment of inspiration. 'The thought of the need of a bank backed by the municipality flashed across my mind one day when crossing Chamberlain Place' (now Chamberlain Square).[3]

Birmingham was the inheritor of a municipal tradition of improvement. Inspired by Chamberlain's father, Joseph, the

Figure 1. Birmingham Municipal Bank, Broad Street - Architect's Drawing, c1930. *Birmingham Reference Library.*

Birmingham Corporation had, during the last quarter of the nineteenth century, taken control of gas, electric and water supplies and initiated a significant programme of urban redevelopment that included Corporation Street.

Neville Chamberlain himself had been an active chairman of the Planning and Public Works Committees, with a strong interest in the provision of housing. He also had an in-depth knowledge of Birmingham's industrial base, through his many business directorships. He was aware of the high wages in the munitions factories, their potentially inflationary effect and the prospect of post-war recession. He also favoured compulsory savings for workers, if only he could '...get the Labour men to give it hearty support'.[4]

Chamberlain had some experience of operating a workers' savings scheme. While managing his father's plantation in the Bahamas during the 1890s, he had founded a savings bank for his native labourers. A similar scheme was being run by Cadburys for their employees at Bournville.

Figure 2. Birmingham Municipal Bank and Masonic Hall, 1930s. *Birmingham Reference Library..*

When Chamberlain became Lord Mayor of Birmingham in November 1915, he concentrated his efforts on effectively organising Birmingham's contribution to the war effort. His main concern was marshalling the savings of the factory workers.

Formal party affiliations did not tie Chamberlain; he occupied a special place in the political spectrum. Although effectively within the Conservative Party, he had an independent regional power-base, centred on Birmingham, and a distinct radical pedigree. Chamberlain was, therefore, in a position to make cross-party alliances, including overtures to the local Labour Party.

The War Savings Bank Committee was formed in November 1915. Prominent among its members were Councillors R R Gelling and Charles Appleby. Most important, however, was the Labour Councillor Eldred Hallas, who provided a direct link to the local trade union movement. Hallas was an eloquent and active campaigner, who was to be Chamberlain's 'best ally over the Bank'.[5]

Birmingham versus Whitehall and the Banks

Birmingham City Council lacked the legal powers to put the scheme into effect. Chamberlain therefore presented the idea to the Treasury. Edwin Montagu, the Financial Secretary, considered the proposal. He rejected the idea in February 1916, on the grounds that the new Bank would be in direct competition with the Treasury for funds.

Chamberlain was not deterred. His brother Austen was a member of the Cabinet and gave advice on the internal workings of Westminster and Whitehall. In March, Chamberlain argued his case before a Treasury Committee, which included Montagu, Stanley Baldwin (the future Prime Minister) and the Governor of the Bank of England. He later wrote that they 'began by heckling me and finished up by heckling each other'.[6]

A deputation from Birmingham and other City Councils lobbied another Government Department, the Local Government Board, for powers to establish Corporation Savings Banks. The deputation was organised by Chamberlain and Ernest Hiley, Birmingham's Town Clerk. By April 1916 the Local Government Board was prepared to

Figure 3. Birmingham Municipal Bank, Broad Street, 1933. *Birmingham Reference Library.*

give the necessary powers. The Treasury, however, remained unenthusiastic.

On 4 April 1916, Birmingham City Council unilaterally adopted the proposal to create a Corporation Savings Bank. A week later Montagu agreed to bring forward the necessary legislation. The clearing banks opposed the Bill. Their leaders, made their concerns about municipal competition for savings known to the Chancellor, McKenna. The Bill was withdrawn after its first reading.

Chamberlain was frustrated by the attitude of the Treasury, but still confident of ultimate success, because he knew that the bankers' reservations were largely unfounded. He wrote to his sister Hilda, saying:

> *I feel somehow that we shall get the thing through, but what is one to say of the Treasury who make no attempt whatever to overcome opposition.*[7]

Chamberlain initiated a publicity campaign in the Birmingham press. He met with the bankers, in an attempt to overcome their concerns. He also used blackmail, warning that

> *...it would be most unfortunate if the banks could be represented in public as opposing a great patriotic movement for purely selfish reasons.*

The bankers were persuaded to acquiesce, but other problems were to arise closer to home.

At a meeting of Birmingham trade unions organised by Eldred Hallas, union representatives attacked the Bank scheme. They were afraid of employers knowing the levels of their members' savings, because this might affect future wage negotiations.

> *I'm beat, wrote Chamberlain, and the Savings bank is dead. The selfishness of the banks and the apathy of the Treasury together make an impenetrable entanglement, but what makes it impossible to carry on fighting is that I have been taken in the rear.*[8]

All was not lost. The Chamberlain family 'click' was at work. Austen Chamberlain had been supporting his brother's case with Cabinet colleagues, while old allies of Joseph Chamberlain, argued the case for Municipal Banks in the House of Lords. Finally, the bankers gave their support to a modified version of Chamberlain's proposal.

In Birmingham, Hallas held meetings with individual trade union leaders and secured their support. Finally, Chamberlain met with

Figure 4. Birmingham Municipal Bank and Hall of Memory, 1946. *Birmingham Reference Library.*

McKenna, Montagu and the Permanent Secretary to the Treasury. A second Bill was introduced to the House of Commons on 12 July 1916.

The powers contained in the new Bill were far more limited than Chamberlain had desired. This reflected the concerns expressed by the banks. The Bill would only apply to local authorities with

Figure 5. Interior of the Municipal Bank, Broad Street, 1953. *Birmingham Reference Library.*

populations of 250,000 or over. All municipal banks were to be closed within three months of the end of the War. Deposits were only to be accepted from the wages of employed people. The maximum level of deposit in an individual account was to be £200. Withdrawals on demand would be limited to £1. Finally, the Banks' investments were to be controlled by the National Debt Commissioners.

Chamberlain nonetheless, recognised this as a bridgehead in establishing the principle of municipal banks. He declared at a public meeting,

...if it is really shown to meet a local need, not all the bankers in Lombard Street will prevent it becoming permanent part of the municipal undertaking.[9]

Birmingham Corporation Savings Bank, a War Time Measure?

The *Municipal Savings Banks (War Loan Investment) Act* became law on 23 August 1916. It had taken Chamberlain and his colleagues ten months of hard negotiation and behind the scenes manoeuvring to achieve this compromise position.

The Bank's offices were established in the basement of the Council's Water Department, in Edmund Street. A wooden counter five yards long and a screen nine feet by five feet were erected. These have remained there to this day, their original purpose largely unrecognised.

A General Manager, John P Hilton, was appointed, from the Yorkshire Penny Bank, on a salary of £500 per annum.[10] He took up office in September 1916 and was to remain there until his retirement in 1946. Other staff were recruited mainly from among existing employees of the City Treasurer's Department. A local firm of accountants, Agar, Bates, Neal & Co of Edmund Street, was engaged as Auditors.

A circular was sent to all Council employees informing them about the new Bank and advising them of the arrangements for saving via salary deductions. An advertising campaign was launched in the Birmingham Mail. This was combined with a lottery for depositors, with prizes donated by local businessmen. The Birmingham Corporation Savings Bank was officially opened on 29 September 1916.

During October 1916 Chamberlain and Hallas were particularly active in promoting the Bank. They addressed meetings at munitions factories. Chamberlain made twelve speeches at factories in twelve days, including at BSA, Cadbury's and Kynoch's. BSA alone produced over 1000 depositors in the first month, with an average weekly saving of more than five shillings.

Hallas attended over a thousand meetings during the first six months of the Bank's existence. He emphasised the patriotic duty to save and the importance of savings to the individual once the War was over, when the munitions would no longer be required and the servicemen returned. 'Can you allow them to enter your houses to a bare cupboard and an empty larder'.[11] Hallas and Chamberlain were

Figure 6. Municipal Bank, Broad Street from Centenary Square, 1998.
C J Brockie.

thus already considering the practicalities of creating a Birmingham '...fit for heroes'.

The Corporation Savings Bank operated through the use of Savings Coupons. The Bank produced coupons valued at one shilling. They were sold to employers on a regular basis. Employers issued the coupons to employees instead of an agreed portion of their wages. Additional coupons could also be purchased from the employer. The coupons were gummed to cards held by the employer, until the value of £1 was reached. The completed cards were then credited against the individual's account at the Bank.

This system had the advantage of placing much of the administrative burden on the employers. It also insured a reasonable degree of privacy for depositors, from their employers, their managers and in many cases, their wives! Factory branches sprang up across Birmingham, including at: the Austin Motor Co, BSA, the Dunlop Rubber Co, GKN, the Wolseley Motor Co, and all City Council Departments. One company, Cadbury's transformed their existing saving scheme to co-operate with the Bank.

Chamberlain's war work in Birmingham was recognised nationally. The incoming Prime Minister, Lloyd George, appointed him to the post of Director of National Service. In January 1917, Chamberlain resigned as Lord Mayor and Chairman of the Savings Bank Committee.

The new Lord Mayor of Birmingham, Alderman Sir David Brooks, assumed chairmanship of the Committee. Much of the political organisation work was carried out by Eldred Hallas and Charles Appleby. They continued the promotional campaign, cultivated employers and resisted frequent Treasury interference.

Figure 7. Municipal Bank, Broad Street, 1998. *C J Brockie.*

Figure 8. Former Acocks Green Branch, Warwick Road. *C J Brockie.*

The Bank and War Savings

The Savings Bank Committee had announced its intention to pay depositors an interest rate of 3.5 per cent. This was based on interest receivable on War Loan investments of five per cent. The National Debt Commissioners, who had oversight of the use of the Bank's funds, chose to limit investments low interest Treasury bills. The consequence was that much lower rates of interest were available to the Bank than had originally been envisaged.

As it transpired, interest on investments paid by the Treasury was progressively reduced from five per cent in 1916 to 3.5 per cent by 1918. The City Council had promoted the Savings Bank's scheme to the people of Birmingham on the basis of a 3.5 per cent interest rate. The payment of such a high rate of interest to depositors, in relation to the interest receivable on investments, left little money to finance the operation of the Bank.

The City Council resolved on 'keeping faith with depositors' and guaranteed the interest rate at 3.5 per cent. Any losses accruing from the operation of the Bank were to be met temporarily from the Rate Fund. This decision was popular with depositors, but not with the Treasury. The Treasury, made repeated attempts between December 1916 and January 1919 to pressure Birmingham City Council into cutting the rate to depositors.[12]

During the first three months of its existence the Corporation Savings Bank attracted £18,000 worth of deposits. In August 1917 the government authorised another War Loan for £250 million. Birmingham City Council contributed £1 million and used the facilities of the Bank to encourage and enable private investment. Similar support was given when new war loans were issued in July 1918 and June 1919.

The Bank also made a contribution to the financing of the war effort through the support of specific campaigns. It raised £26.4 million for the government.

'Homes Fit for Heroes'?
Chamberlain's brief period as Director of National Service ended in failure. He lacked support from the Prime Minister and also faced the opposition of other ministers. He resumed his place on the

Figure 9. Former Ladywood Branch, now a bookmaker's, 1998. *C J Brockie.*

Savings Bank Committee and was also adopted as the Conservative and Unionist Parliamentary Candidate for Ladywood.

The Prime Minister, Lloyd George had declared the need to build homes 'fit for the heroes who have won the war'. It had been estimated that there were 400,000 houses in Britain that were unfit for human habitation. There was also the issue of overcrowding. An enquiry carried out by Birmingham City Council in 1913 had highlighted local housing problems.

Chamberlain stated his views on housing policy during the 1918 General Election campaign.

> *The proper way to deal with the question was for the State to take it up, to provide the money, and announce at once to the people a great programme of national housing - not to be undertaken by the State itself, but to be carried out by the local authorities which alone knew the conditions, could provide sites and could collect rents in trust for the State.*[13]

Figure 10. Former Stechford Branch, Station Road *C J Brockie.*

In 1919 Neville Chamberlain resumed the Chairmanship of the Savings Bank Committee. The Versailles Peace Conference was now in progress. This meant that the Corporation Savings Bank had only a few months of life left to it under the legislation.

Birmingham City Council resolved to seek the necessary powers to maintain the Bank on a permanent basis, through a Private Bill. This proposed that the Bank should be run as a savings bank, abandoning the coupon system and operating through branches. In addition to offering facilities for saving, the new bank would advance money on the mortgages of houses within the City and loan surplus funds to the Council. The Bill was brought before Parliament in June 1919.

Chamberlain addressed the Commons in support of the Bill. He criticised the constraints placed on the Bank's operations during the War. He estimated that three quarters of the money placed with the Bank would not otherwise have been saved and attributed this to public confidence in the City Council. He concluded 'if after the war 50,000 have saved £5 each through the bank then Birmingham would have again shown the way to the Country'.[14]

The *Birmingham Corporation Act* received assent on 15 August 1919. This enabled the creation of two new Council Departments, Municipal Bank and Housing. The Bank came under the control of the newly re-titled Municipal Bank Management Committee, chaired by Charles Appleby.

The powers granted for the operation of the Municipal Bank were less restrictive than previously. The most important change, however, was that the Municipal Bank was to be a permanent City Council service.

The Corporation Savings Bank finally closed on 17 November 1919. It had been a qualified success. Nearly 24,500 accounts had been operated, £600,000 worth of deposits received and £295,000 worth of withdrawals processed, during the three years that the Bank had been open. It was the only savings bank to have been created under the 1916 legislation.

The Bank Committee had reported in July 1919, that

> *a remarkable feature is the stability of the accounts opened by the early depositors, showing that the desire to save is not a passing fancy, but the expression of a powerful instinct which will continue to act so long as the people are provided with facilities suited to their habits and conditions.*

These were notable achievements.

The Birmingham Municipal Bank opened on 1 September 1919. The head office was in The Council House, with seventeen branches across Birmingham. A logo displaying a key was designed and together with the motto 'Security with Interest', became the symbol of the Municipal Bank. Posters with the slogans 'Simplicity! Security! Safety!' and 'Join your own City's Bank' were displayed on Corporation buses and trams. This extensive marketing of a Council service was innovative.

Over ninety-three per cent of accounts were transferred from the old Savings Bank to the new Municipal Bank. Temporary branches were also established to test local demand around Birmingham. Premises were rented for these branch offices, including shops and licence-less pubs, like the *Highland Laddie* inn, Duddeston. Existing Council Offices were also used, including libraries and public baths.

The *Birmingham Corporation Act* had given the Municipal Bank a new specific power to grant home loans. Home purchase loans would now be available through the Municipal Bank, for: assistance of up to eighty per cent of the cost of the purchase of houses within the City, to depositors with the Bank, up to a value of £1,000 per loan.

Two new, but separately established services were brought under the auspices of the Bank. These were the *School Savings Banks Scheme* and the *Allotments Loans Scheme*. School savings banks in Birmingham had been established in July 1915. When the sum saved by a pupil had reached £1 that amount was automatically transferred to an interest-bearing account at the Municipal Bank.

Housing was, however, the sphere in which Birmingham and national policy making were most closely aligned. The *Housing and Town Planning Act 1919*, allowed for local authorities to provide a housing subsidy in excess of a penny rate. Between 1919 and 1921 some 209,000 houses were built nationally. In Birmingham 3,234 houses were built, at a cost of between £900 and £1,000 each.

The collapse of the Lloyd George coalition in 1922 provided a political stepping-stone for Neville Chamberlain. He eventually became Minister of Health in the Conservative Government. As the minister responsible for housing, Chamberlain brought forward new legislation, the *Housing Act 1923*. This provided subsidies for private builders and local authorities. Between 1923 and 1928 some 8,263 houses were built in Birmingham, using Chamberlain's subsidy.[15]

Properties on the new housing estates at Acocks Green, Alum Rock, Bordesley Green, Billesley, Erdington, Fox Hollies, Hay Mills, Kings Heath, Pype Hayes, Short Heath, Small Heath and Ward End, were made available for purchase. The Housing Department, in

Figure 11. Former Ward End Branch, Washwood Heath Road. *C J Brockie.*

conjunction with the Municipal Bank, produced an information booklet for tenants entitled 'How to be your own landlord' in 1925. Between 1923 and 1929 some 3,314 council houses, at a capital value of nearly £1.3 million were sold. The Municipal Bank had advanced more than £1 million towards this.

Birmingham City Council introduced a 'Progressive Mortgage Scheme' to support the building of new houses. Between 1923 and 1931 mortgages to the value of £516,951 were provided under the scheme. This represented ninety per cent of the building cost of 1,377 new houses. The cost of buying a house in Birmingham, during the 1920s, was, however, nearly twice that of renting.

In 1921 the City Council's Water Department, in whose premises the Municipal Bank's head office was based, made provision for depositors to pay their water bills through the Bank. By 1926 Electricity, Gas, Salvage and Rates were offering the same facilities to Bank depositors. This enabled the local payment of Council service charges through the branches of the Bank.[16]

'Home Safes' were introduced in December 1922 to support small scale 'penny saving' at home. This was based on the 'piggy bank'. The Bank Committee arranged for the Home Safes to be designed and manufactured in Birmingham. During the first four months of 1923 some 2,469 Home Safes were issued. By 1933 this had increased to 80,315, with £212,021 15s 6d being deposited in that year.

A new head office for the Bank was opened in Edmund Street in July 1925. Known as 'Swissles', this was formerly the premises of the Nestle Swiss Chocolate Company. Chamberlain, who was again Minister of Health, performed the ceremony.

The growth in savings at the Municipal Bank was to continue to grow throughout the 1920s. By March 1929, over 280,000 Birmingham people had accounts with the Bank, with balances totalling nearly £10.3 million. During that year the Bank had handled 1.6 million transactions, made-up of £4.6 million worth of deposits and £3.7 million worth of withdrawals.

The Municipal Bank had become established as one of Birmingham City Council's services. It was also the only savings institution empowered to make loans. Chamberlain set out his own philosophy in a speech, in March 1929. In direct reference to the Bank, he said 'one has only to compare the methods say of the Municipal Bank in Birmingham with those of the Savings Bank or the Post Office to see an entirely different scheme of keeping in touch with the public'.[17]

Extension of Birmingham's Powers

The Municipal Bank continued to develop and expand during the 1930s. A New Head Office in Broad Street was planned, as part of the proposed Civic Centre, (which included Baskerville House). It was built in Portland Stone with ionic columns and decorated with Egyptian symbols depicting labour, perseverance, commerce, integrity, industry, progress, banking and finance. It cost £85,000 to build.

Chamberlain laid the foundation stone in October 1932 and the premises were opened by HRH the Duke of Kent in November 1933. In his speech the Duke said:

The success of the Bank is clearly due to its own intrinsic merits-to the fact that it meets a public need; that it is, in fact, part of the city's administration, backed by the security of the rates.[18]

It is noteworthy that the Treasury had viewed this as an argument against extending municipal banks.

The new premises provided a high prestige headquarters for the Bank. It also provided facilities for new services to depositors. There was safe deposit beneath the Banking Hall, which provided 1,320 individual depositories in four sizes. By 1946 the number of safe deposits had been increased to 4,640 to keep pace with demand.

The *Birmingham Corporation (General Powers) Act 1929* had given Birmingham the power to open branches of the Bank in neighbouring local authority areas. The first was opened in Oldbury in 1932. Four such branches were in operation by 1935. In 1935 a branch was established in Solihull. In the following year a branch was opened in Sutton Coldfield.

The *Birmingham Corporation Act 1935* was another landmark for the Bank. This allowed for the provision of loans to depositors for the purchase of houses in adjoining local authorities. It also authorised loans for home repairs and improvements. In 1931 there were 6,800 mortgages in force with a value of over £1.8 million. The number of new mortgages advanced declined during the depression years of the early 1930s. By 1937 some 7,700 mortgages were active. The number of mortgages reached a peak in 1940 with 8,200 mortgages, having a total value of nearly £2.7 million.

In 1938 Birmingham celebrated the centenary of the founding of the Corporation. Various publications reflected Birmingham's civic achievements. In one, Harrison Barrow, the Chairman of the Municipal Bank Committee wrote: 'there is no doubt that the fact of the Bank being a possession of the citizens of Birmingham, contributes to its continued popularity'.[19]

The Bank during the Second World War
In the spring of 1939 the Municipal Bank Committee agreed to place the excess of deposits over withdrawals with the National Debt Commissioners, in preparation for the coming War. Over £41 million was invested by 1948. Between 1940 and 1948 over £8.6 million worth of National Savings Certificates and government bonds were also purchase through the Bank.

The Bank promoted a number of work based savings schemes, to capture the surplus cash of the munitions workers. These continued after the war as the 'Direct Transfer Scheme'. Schools banks were promoted and the use of the new National Savings Stamp was

Figure 12. Former Yardley Branch, Church Road. *C J Brockie.*

introduced. Balances at the Bank rose from £29.3 million in 1939 to £67.7 million by 1945.

Sir John Anderson, the Chancellor of the Exchequer acknowledged the contribution made by the Municipal Bank to the financing of the war effort, in May 1945:

> *The Bank has taken a very important part in all sides of savings work in the Birmingham Region . . . the National Savings Movement owes much to the hard work and expert knowledge which the officials of the Bank have contributed.*[20]

Encouragement of savings and investment were not the only wartime activities that the Municipal Bank engaged in. The Bank was given responsibility for a range of financial assistance to the civilian population. Over 50,000 children were evacuated, with the Bank arranging for the payment of evacuation fees. The wages of Civil Defence staff were paid through the Bank. From 1941 Home Assistance Allowance, to those made homeless through bombing was paid via the Bank.

New counter services had developed. Midwifery Service fees had become payable through the Bank. Education fees and grants were also administered, as were payments to the Birmingham Hospitals Saturday Fund. These services were only available to depositors, who by 1941 numbered nearly half a million people. From 1941 to 1948 Public Assistance payments were made directly into accounts held at the Bank.

The Post-War Bank in a Changing World

The welfare and nationalisation policies of the post-war Labour Government affected the operation of Birmingham City Council and its Bank. The *National Assistance Act 1948* created the National Assistance Board, removing the last vestiges of the public assistance provision from local government. The special wartime allowances administered by the Bank were also ended in 1948.

Birmingham Council's electricity and gas supply services were nationalised between April 1948 and May 1949. These were services that had made use of the facilities of the Municipal Bank and arrangements were made with the respective regional boards to allow Bank depositors to continue to pay their bills via the Bank.

A major problem faced by the Bank, during and after the war, was the shortage of trained staff. In 1945 the Savings Bank Institute was established as a professional staff association. The Municipal Bank and the largest Trustee Savings Banks each contributed towards establishment of a staff-training organisation. The syllabus included a study of the classic novels The *Master of Ballantrae* and *David Copperfield*. Copies of these novels were apparently unobtainable in post-war Birmingham, much to the concern of Municipal Bank staff.[21]

During the 1950s the Bank continued to co-operate with the Trustee Savings Banks over the promotion of National Savings and staff training. In 1953 most of the Trustee Savings Banks adopted the Municipal Bank's mechanised ledger posting system. The Bank joined the Trustee Savings Bank Credit Transfer System in 1962.

This allowed depositors to use Standing Orders and Credit Transfer facilities.

Between 1945 and 1951 the number of accounts at the Municipal Bank increased by 13 per cent, while the value of deposits increased by twenty-five per cent. A shortage of materials and rationing had limited house building, despite the need for post-war reconstruction. As a result the annual number of new mortgages arranged by the Bank did not return to the pre-war level until 1950.

There was still demand for home ownership, based on the savings accumulated since 1939. By 1956 the annual number of new mortgages issued by the Municipal Bank had exceeded 1,400. This represented an advance to depositors of over £1.5 million, or approximately £2 for every depositor. The total number of mortgages in force was 8,422.

New Accounts, but No New Role!

In 1956 the government initiated a new National Savings drive to recruit two million new savers within two years by giving tax concessions on savings accounts. This was to apply to the Trustee Savings Banks, but not the Municipal Bank.

Birmingham City Council offered to set up a separate department within the Bank paying a fixed rate of interest to depositors of 2.5 per cent, with excess deposits being passed to the National Debt Commissioners for investment. In exchange the government would allow the tax concession to depositors using that account.

Negotiations took place between Birmingham City Council and the Treasury. Birmingham was represented by the Lord Mayor Alderman Apps, the Chairman of the Bank Committee, Councillor I L Morgan and local Labour MPs, including Roy Jenkins. Sir Edward Boyle, who was the Conservative MP for Handsworth, represented the Treasury.

The tax concession was finally given to depositors at the Municipal Bank under the *Finance (No 2) Act 1956*. The 'Savings No 2 Department' came into operation in January 1957. More than £1 million worth of National Savings Certificates were sold through the Bank in 1956. By 1961 the Municipal Bank was contributing over £1.6 million to National Savings.

In 1959 there were 128,030 Home Safes in use. Some £10,264,058 had been deposited via this method since the Home Safes were introduced in 1922. From the 1960s onwards, Home Safes were largely used to encourage children to save.

The level of annual deposits through the schools savings banks doubled during the 1950s to over £58,000. From 1956 onwards, school savings began to decline. Despite a campaign directed at young savers in the mid-1960s, the level of deposits continued to fall, reaching a low point of £29,000 per annum in 1969.

The Municipal Bank introduced new customer services that reflected the affluent society of the early 1960s. The number of safe deposit boxes in use increased from 8,156 in 1956 to 10,405 in 1966. Foreign currency and Travellers' Cheques were supplied through an arrangement with Thomas Cook & Son. The purchase and sale of stocks and shares were arranged on behalf of depositors. Dividends were credited directly to savings accounts.

A major shake-up occurred within the National Savings Movement in 1965, when the Treasury allowed the TSBs to introduced Current Accounts and Cheques. The Municipal Bank Committee began negotiations with the Treasury to introduce Investment Accounts and Current Accounts.

The 'No 3 Investment Department' opened in January 1967. Accounts were limited to those with deposits in excess of £50, in the No 1 Savings Department. One month's notice was required for withdrawals. In July 1967 the 'Current Account Department' began operating. In the first year over 23,000 cheques were cleared, with a value of £465,000. Chequebooks were operated through the TSB's system and cheque guarantee cards were issued in 1969. In the same year 'Save As You Earn' (SAYE) was also introduced.

By 1966 the Municipal Bank had sixty-eight branches in and around Birmingham. This was more than any other bank. In March the prestigious new City Branch, in Martineau Square was opened. The Bank's 'six days opening' policy was, however, under threat. Staffing problems and pressure from the TSB caused the Bank Committee to abandon Saturday opening in July 1969.

The Birmingham Municipal Bank celebrated its golden jubilee in 1969. A commemorative dinner was held in the Head Office, at which Roy Jenkins, now Chancellor of the Exchequer was the guest of honour.[22]

The Process to Merger

The Government's policy of relaxing credit controls increased the level of competition in the Financial Services sector. The Municipal Bank effectively doubled its fund for home loans. An application to the Treasury for powers to make general loans was, however refused.

The future of National Savings and particularly the savings banks looked uncertain. In April 1971, a government Committee, under the chairmanship of Sir Harry Page, the former Treasurer of Manchester City Council, was established.

The committee came out against the existing structure and recommended that:

> *The* [savings] *banks should become banking organisations similar in most respects to the clearing banks, except that they will be mutual and non-profit making, and will confine their activities to the operation of personal accounts.*

The semi-independent Trustee Savings Banks would be consolidated into nine Regional TSBs. The Bank of England would establish a clearing centre for all savings banks, including the Municipal Bank. Ordinary Savings Departments, whose funds were invested by the National Debt Commissioners, would be converted to deposit accounts.

In June 1973 the Central TSB Ltd. was set-up as the clearing centre and the process of amalgamating the individual TSBs began. The Municipal Bank was already co-operating with the Midland TSB on the development of computer systems. In 1972 the Bank had joined the computer consortium, which produced systems for accounting, costing and management services.

In early 1974 the Municipal Bank Committee discussed the possibility of amalgamation with the TSB. Conservative Councillors in particular were keen to see the Bank operate on a full commercial basis. The Municipal Bank was kept informed of the TSB's on going negotiations with the Treasury.

On 23 June 1975 the Lord Mayor, Councillor Albert Jackson, opened a new branch of the Bank at Boldmere Road, Sutton Coldfield. Although another branch was planned for Four Oaks, this was to be the last new branch of the Birmingham Municipal Bank.

The *Trustee Savings Bank Act 1976* laid down a programme to develop the Trustee Savings Banks to full commercial status. The TSB would be free from direct Treasury control and all funds held by the National Debt Commissioners would be returned. Despite the Page Committee's recommendation, there was no mention of 'mutual' status in the legislation.

The Municipal Bank Committee unanimously decided that the Bank should not remain outside the TSB organisation. It would merge with Coventry, Walsall and Wolverhampton TSBs.

The Birmingham Municipal Bank closed its doors on 31 March

1976 and on the following day a new bank, the Birmingham Municipal Trustee Savings Bank, opened for business.

Birmingham City Councillors had acquiesced in the end of a municipal experiment that had lasted sixty years. The Municipal Bank closed with reserves of £6.5 million and assets of £146 million. The number of account holders stood at 786,330, for a population of just over a million people.

Councillor Norman Hargreaves the last chairman of the Bank Committee and first Chairman of the board of trustees came to regret the merger, describing it as a 'most retrograde step' in a letter to *The Times*.[24] His colleagues did not share this view and he was removed as Chairman of the Trustees in 1977. His successor, Councillor Denis Martineau went on to become a director of the TSB when it was finally privatised in 1985.

All that remains today, apart from the former head-office building in Broad Street, is the 'Iron Man' statute in Victoria Square. This was a gift to the people of Birmingham from TSB, before they too were taken-over by Lloyds Bank.

Notes and References

1 Feilig, K *Life of Neville Chamberlain*, London: Macmillan, 1970, p60.

2 Briggs A *History of Birmingham, Vol 11: Borough and City 1865-1938*, London: Oxford University Press, 1952.

3 Jones, J T *History of the Corporation of Birmingham, Vol V: 1915-193.* Birmingham City Council General Purposes Committee, 1940, p461.

4 Dilks, D *Neville Chamberlain, Vol I: Pioneering and Reform 1869-192*, Cambridge University Press 1984, p158.

5 Feilig, K p61.

6 *Ibid* p60.

7 *Ibid* p60.

8 *Ibid* p60.

9 *Ibid* p61.

10 Hilton, J P *Britain's First Municipal Savings Bank: the Romance of a great Achievement*, Birmingham: Blackfriars Press, 1927.

11 Dilks, D. *ibid* p178.

12 Jones, J T *ibid.*

13 Macleod, I *Neville Chamberlain*, London: Muller, 1961, p77.

14 *Ibid* p49.

15 Chinn, C *Homes for People: 100 years of Council Housing in Birmingham*, Exeter: Birmingham Books, 1991.

16 Jones, J T *ibid.*

17 Chamberlain, N, The management of Public Utility Undertakings Public Administration, *Vol 7* pp103-110.

18 Jones, S T *ibid.* p468.

19 Barrow, H, The Municipal Bank, an example to the nation, the *Birmingham Gazette* Centenary Celebration Supplement, 1938

20 Black, H J *History of the Corporation of Birmingham Vol VI : 1936-1950* Birmingham: Birmingham City Council General Purposes Committee, 1957.

21 Moss, M and Russell, I *An Invaluable Treasurer: A History of the TSB*, London: Weidenfeld and

Nicholson, 1994, p203.
22 Birmingham City Council *Birmingham Municipal Bank Golden jubilee 1919-1969*, Birmingham: Birmingham City Council Municipal Bank Committee, 1969.
23 Moss, M and Russell, I *ibid.*, p 275.
24 *Ibid* p 284.

Bibliography

Primary Sources:
1. Birmingham City Council, *Minutes of the (War) Savings Bank Committee*, 1916-1919.
2. Birmingham City Council, *Minutes of the Municipal Bank Committee*, 1919-1976.
3. Birmingham City Council, *Birmingham Municipal Bank Annual Reports*, 1920-1958.
4. Birmingham City Council, *Birmingham Municipal Bank Annual Reports*, 1959-1976.

Secondary Sources:
1. Montgomery, Hyde H *Neville Chamberlain*, London: Weidenfeld and Nicholson, 1976.
2. Sutcliffe, A and Smith, R *History of Birmingham, Vol III, 1939-1970*, London: Oxford University Press, 1974.
3. Upton, C.A. *History of Birmingham*, Chichester: Phillimore, 1993.

Journal Articles:
1. Hilton, J.P. The Birmingham Municipal Bank, *The Banker*, Vol 8, 1926, pp 3-8.
2. Hopkins, E Working Class life in Birmingham between the Wars, 1918-1939 *Midland History* Vol 15, 1990, pp 129-150.

8. THE BIRMINGHAM MISSION

by Ann Firth

DURING THE VICTORIAN ERA non-conformist churches helped provide much needed aid to the poor, in what seems to have been a two-way relationship offering benefits to all. The church offered food, clothing, shelter and healthcare and, in return, they received the poorís trust, faith and gratitude which inevitably led to increased attendances at Sunday services, conversions and memberships. (Figure 1)

Many churches soon found their buildings inadequate. They could not cope with increased demands for space, so some hired extra rooms at other venues, some considered extensions and others built a new larger church.

Figure 1. Methodist Central Hall, 1953. *Birmingham Reference Library.*

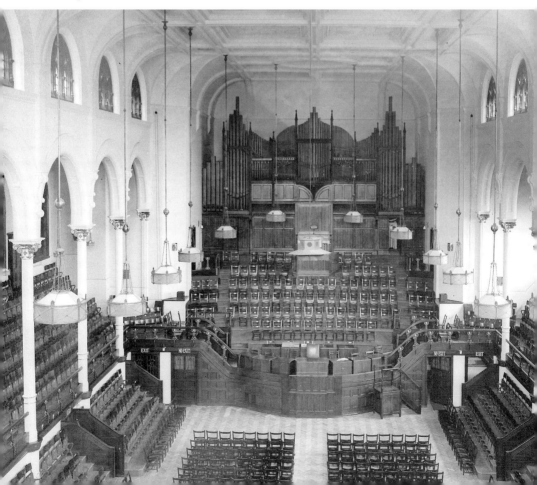

John Wesley, founder of Methodist churches, had acquired freehold land in Cherry Street in 1782 and built a little chapel which he opened on 7 July 1782. One hundred years later, Birmingham Council put a compulsory purchase order on this building, thus providing the means to enable the trustees to build their larger church elsewhere.

The new church could hold one thousand worshippers. It stood in Lower Priory and was called the Central Hall. The Methodist Conference elected a minister, well known for his musical talents, to lead the Birmingham Mission, the Reverend Luke Wiseman. It opened on 8 September 1887. Mission work flourished and within ten years the Hall was having to hire the large room at the Midland Institute for Sunday services as well as providing them at the Hall. Trustees were again faced with finding more space.

The Corporation Scheme to clear the city of some of its worst slums meant that land was now available opposite the law courts. The Reverend Luke Wiseman had previously opposed plans to build a theatre there. Now he had a new interest in the site. The new Central Hall opened on 16 September 1903 in what is now called Corporation Street. The Methodist Conference had decided some years before that its churches should be beautiful places, especially, its Hall. It did not feel that the gin palaces should be the only places that offered decoration and beauty.

The main worship area of the Hall has ornate columns floor to ceiling. Two stained glass windows are at the back, while at the front is a unique German organ with rows of seats in front for the choir. The room is enormous and very beautiful. It has a narrow corridor on the outside, encircling it on three sides with mosaic walls and floors. Small rooms lead off at right angles to the corridor which were used for all the Hall's various works. The small rooms, a large hall and kitchen facilities were available for hire to help offset the Mission's costs. Mission work was varied, projects grew, projects changed, new ideas came along, increasing needs meant the Mission had to flexible and quick to respond.

Work was not confined to within the city but branched out to areas of Aston, Nechells and Hockley. In the early nineties it also worked in areas of Kingsbury, Kingstanding, Perry Common and Ladywood, and later in Alvechurch, Tysley and Sheldon.

Shaftesbury House

Excessive overcrowding in homes often led to older children being forced out to fend for themselves. Young girls in this situation could

Figure 2. Shaftesbury House, St Mary's Row, 1932. *Birmingham Reference Library.*

Figure 3. Sitting Room at Shaftesbury House, 1932. *Birmingham Reference Library.*
Figure 4. Dining Room at Shaftesbury House, 1932. *Birmingham Reference Library.*

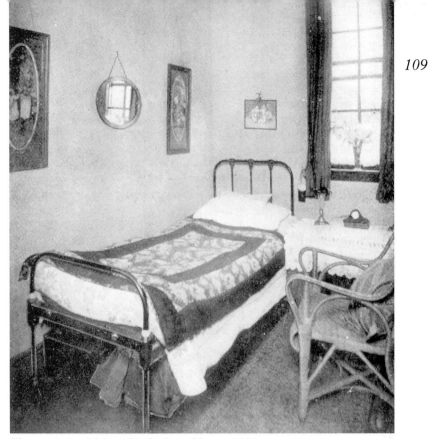

Figure 5. A cubicle at Shaftesbury House, 1932. *Birmingham Reference Library.*
Figure 6. The Laundry at Shaftesbury House, 1932. *Birmingham Reference Library.*

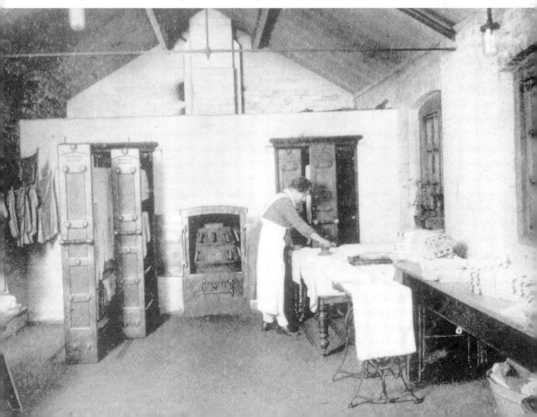

find refuge at Shaftesbury House. Many hundreds preferred this to the alternatives on offer such as begging and prostitution. The average wage in the early 1900s for a young girl was around seven shillings and sixpence (37.5p).

In 1905 the cost of three meals a day, laundry facilities, own bed, care and friendship at the house, was five shillings (25p). The original house could only accommodate sixteen girls at a time. The Mission was concerned about all the others. Where could they go? Affluent and influential people of the day, such as George Cadbury, met with the Reverend Wiseman, appeals were made and the money came pouring in. The Lord Mayor opened the new house on 28 November 1912.

The converted warehouse provided accommodation for one hundred girls at a time. The address was 6 St Mary's Row. It was opposite St Mary's Church. The area is now under the Dental Hospital. Shaftesbury House still exists today in the Moseley area. It is now under the guidance and care of Social Services and houses only six girls at a time.

Newton House

Destitute men could find shelter at Newton House in Newton Street which opened in 1901. The cost was sixpence a night for a clean bed and washing facilities. No food was provided, though facilities to cook their own were. The house was in the charge of Mr Tom Broomhall who believed that cleanliness was next to godliness. Any man that came in dirty was made to wash before being given a bed or being allowed to sit in the warm sitting room. Accommodation was for thirty-three men at a time. It closed in 1904 (see paragraph on *Sea Horse Tavern*).

Sea Horse Tavern

Drunkenness was a serious social problem not only of adults but of children as well. One of the worst of the seven hundred public houses in Birmingham was the *Sea Horse*. Visited mainly by thieves, prostitutes and murderers, it is claimed that many crimes were planned and arranged there. The Mission took over the tavern and turned it into a social club and coffeehouse. People alive today remember the concerts, singalongs and meetings that were held there nightly. Some remember living near and listening to the music. In 1904 the Mission closed Newton House and provided accommodation here instead. The *Sea Horse* was in Buck Street. The area is now under Aston University.

Labour Yard

Attached to the *Sea Horse* was the labour yard/ woodyard. Strike after strike leading up to the 1914 war meant many families were facing starvation. Help and work could be found here each afternoon for twenty-two men, providing wages for them and a little income for the mission. Records for 1901 show the sale of bundles of wood for the year was 277,000. Payment to the men was by weight of wood chopped. The Mission did not offer work in the mornings in order to give men the opportunity to look for a day's work elsewhere. The workhouse would detain men in the mornings and release them in the afternoons to look for work, when normally a day's work would already have been given out. It appears that that the Mission got it the right way round.

Havergal House

This girls' club (later open to boys) was in Hatchett Street, opposite Newtown Row Chapel. It opened around 1890 and was a place for factory girls, young and old to socialise. Apart from prayer meetings the club also offered opportunities to learn to knit and sew. Surrounding the house were dirty courtyards, the results of endless black smoke from numerous chimneys bellowing out continuously day and night. All this smoke was poisoning the air, along with the putrid smells caused through bad sanitation. It is no wonder that outings to the Lickey Hills or the seaside were popular and well supported. Havergal continued until the 1960s when the premises were sold to the Boys' Brigade. The capital sum realised by the sale was invested and proceeds are still being used to support work with young people in Birmingham.

After the depression of the 1880s there were 11,000 paupers living in Birmingham. Many Victorians thought charity work was a well-meaning diversion for middle-class do-gooders, especially the women. Even so, by the

Figure 7. The new Havergal House, 1936. *Birmingham Reference Library.*

Figure 8. The Lord Mayor, Lady Mayoress and Lady Stamp in the New Havergal House, 1936. *Birmingham Reference Library.*

Figure 9. Cookery Classes, Havergal House, 1936. *Birmingham Reference Library.*

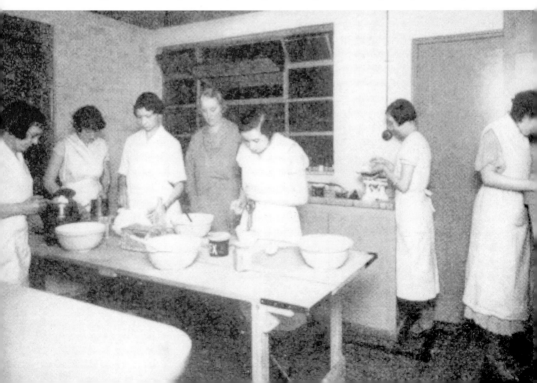

Figure 10. The Roof Garden, Havergal House, 1936. *Birmingham Reference Library.*

end of the nineteenth century a quarter of the relief needed was given by charities. Birmingham now had a reputation as a forward thinking city regarding housing, education and transport. It is doubtful if this meant much to those who daily survived the torments of hunger, illness and early death. Doctors who gave their services free were available at the Hall two mornings a week. The costs of medication were kept low and were free to those who could not afford them.

Ragged Schools were well attended by many children. This was probably the only education they ever received apart from that gained in the Sunday School. The term 'Ragged School' was changed around 1900 to 'Children's Mission'. The report of 1905 states 2000 children in one room with 380 in the Children's Service in another room. Prizes were given at the end of each year for attendance or conduct.

Central Hall

The basement of the Hall is a maze of corridors with doors leading to what are now shops on the frontage. These corridors were open to provide shelter with hot chocolate and toast to the beggars and street sellers. The Hall was open day and night for religious services and prayer groups as well as temperance meetings, Boys' Brigade, Girls' clubs, Mothers' meetings, singing, drama, knitting, sewing, etc. The Mothers' meetings started a savings club and a clothing club. Money saved could go towards medical expenses or food when there was no work. Anyone donating to the clothing club would regularly be given clothes or material to make their own.

Staff at the Hall were also available at night. They were often asked to sit with a dying person and to give words of comfort to the bereaved. Sisters were often asked to be present at the birth of a

Figure 11. Windows at the back of the church. *A. Firth.*

child. Mission work had no set hours. It went on day and night.

The Hall had many churches attached to it including Nechells Hall, Cecil Hall, Lichfield Road. Two churches worthy of special mention are Bradford Street and Newtown Row Chapel. Bradford Street was the oldest Wesleyan Chapel in Birmingham. John Wesley wrote in his journal on 12 July 1786, 'At noon I preached in the new chapel at Deritend. To build one here was an act of mercy indeed.' The premises Wesley wrote of became schoolrooms when a new chapel was built in 1822. Deritend was then surrounded with a poverty-stricken community. Workers in the church came in from outside areas to give not only their service but also their money to help with the Mission's work. The church closed on 19 October 1936 when 124 members were transferred to other churches.

Newtown Row Chapel could be regarded as having been the first branch of the Central hall according to the 1902 Report. The Reverend J Gregory took over the deserted chapel and within six months it became a 'hive of Christian industry with notorious characters converted'. Midnight services reached the people who normally spent their time in the pubs. Mission staff visited every pub in the city inviting everyone to their services. Before a service there would be a half an hour singing in the streets to encourage people to go inside. What a congregation they had – drunks by the hundreds, criminals, prostitutes, bookies, gamblers and even publicans that brought their customers along. The church survived until it was bombed in the Second World War.

In 1913 the Reverend Luke Wiseman wrote 'No part of the Mission suffers more than the Central Hall from the steady stream of migration to the suburbs.' By 1933 prominent workers in the Mission found their skills no longer needed so had to look elsewhere for work. In 1937 there was a widespread reduction in the numbers of children attending Sunday Schools which coincided with further increases in drunkenness in young people. The Mission was working out how to tackle this when war broke out again. Thankfully the Hall survived the bombings but the city was in ruins and it was many years before it was rebuilt. People

Figure 12. Methodist Central Hall Tower, 1998. *A. Firth.*

Figure 13. Methodist Central Hall, 1998. *A. Firth.*

had now moved out of the city and the Mission faced a depopulated centre.

In 1948 Mr Joseph Alexander Patrick gave the Mission twenty-two acres of woodland near Alvechurch to be used for 'the general well-being of society'. The Mission arranged holidays at this site for hundreds of Birmingham children before it passed into the hands and safekeeping of the Redditch Circuit in the early nineties.

16 February 1980 was the opening day of the Law Courts Family Centre based at the Hall. The centre is still open today continuing to provide care for young children while their parents/ carers attend the courts.

High Spot, a drop-in centre for the homeless opened in September 1981. When the Hall was sold in 1988 and the congregation moved to new premises, the High Spot moved with them changing its name

Figure 14. Part of mural in foyer of Central Hall depicting other city centre views including Tower on left. *A. Firth.*

Figure 15. Part of mural on wall on foyer of Central hall depicting Corporating Street. *A. Firth.*

to the Bridge. Unfortunately this project closed in the nineties.

Share Care 1 was a small charity shop in Ryder Street based in one of the Hall's own units. It opened in Autumn 1980 and closed after about seven years through lack of volunteers and failure to meet Health and Safety requirements.

Today the tall majestic tower of the Hall still stands proud though not many people realise why. The blue illuminated cross was taken down shortly after its sale in 1988 though the large letters that spell out its name still survive. By looking closely a small balcony can be seen at the top of the tower. A fine view of Birmingham can be gained by climbing many straight ladders bolted to the walls. There is also grass and dandelions on the balcony, the roofs, walls and broken upstairs windows. The place looks derelict. Since its sale it has played host to boxing events and is now the venue for night 'raves' on three evenings a week.

The Central hall congregation is today based in the Central Methodist Church only a few yards down from the grand arched door of the Hall. The Chinese Christian Church is also based there which means the church can be open longer. The staff sit on many committees involved in working with the homeless, people with special needs, prison visiting, hospital visiting and religious rallies.

The Reverend Luke Wiseman was a strong temperance man. He often visited the courts to stop public houses getting a licence or renewing one. A few yards from the Hall is *Yates Wine Lodge*. One cannot help but wonder what he and Joseph Chamberlain, who built Corporation Street and himself a strong temperance person, would think of the mottoes above the windows of the Wine Lodge 'a day without wine is a day without sunshine' and the real sting in the tail 'Moderation is true temperance'.

Sources

1. Sugden, H.J. *What I saw in the Birmingham Mission*. 1902.
2. Armitage, R *Mission in the Second City*, 1987.

Other information gained from personal interviews with past and present members of the Central Methodist Church and from Birmingham Library Service, Archives Department.

9. Monumental Soldier

by Roger Ward

IN THE GROUNDS OF ST PHILIP'S CATHEDRAL, a few yards from Temple Row, in one of the busiest and most pleasant quarters of central Birmingham, stands an impressive monument. A handsome obelisk of Portland stone, it soars nearly fifty feet into the Birmingham sky. On the south face of the base is carved the head and shoulders of an imposing, moustached figure whose braided tunic, and the military regalia and acanthus leaves carved above his

Figure 1a. Detail from the monument erected in memory of the late Colonel Burnaby. *R. Ward.*

Figure 1b. The memorial to the late Colonel Burnaby, erected in St Philip's Church, Birmingham. *R. Ward.*

head, identify him as a soldier. On the north face of the base is carved the name of this hero figure – BURNABY. The monument scorns further identification, except that on the east face is carved KHIVA 1875 and on the west ABU KLEA 1885. One suspects that very few of the many passers-by, or those who rest awhile on benches around the monument, could identify the man so arrogantly commemorated, let alone the significance or the location of the places named.

Who was Burnaby? Where and what were Khiva and Abu Klea? What was Burnaby's connection with Birmingham? Who raised this monument and for what purpose?

Frederick Gustavus Burnaby was one of the most remarkable figures of the Victorian age. Soldier, adventurer, travel writer, pioneer, politician, he had by the time of his death in 1885 become a household name.[1] Born in 1842, the son of a country parson, he was educated at Bedford School, at Harrow, and privately in Germany. In 1859, at the tender age of seventeen, he was gazetted as a cornet in the Household Brigade, rising steadily through the commissioned ranks to become colonel of the Royal Horseguards in 1884. Standing six feet four inches tall and weighing over fifteen stone, Burnaby was reputed to be the strongest man in the British army. His feats of strength were legendary, including the ability to lift two ponies, one under each arm. His regiment, known as the Blues, was a highly fashionable one and its officers moved easily among the elite of Victorian society. On one occasion, while entertaining the Prince of Wales in the regimental mess, Burnaby is reputed to have wrapped a poker around the royal neck. A painting of Burnaby in the National Portrait Gallery by J G Tissot is dated 1870 and suggests that he was already a well known figure, at least in high society, at a comparatively young age.[2]

Burnaby, however, was no mere gladiator. He was reputed to speak at least seven languages, including Russian, Turkish and Arabic. He was also an accomplished writer who contributed to *Vanity Fair* and the *Times*, for which newspaper he covered the Carlist wars in Spain in the early 1870s. But most of all he became celebrated for his travel writing, authoring two books which became instant best sellers, were to be many times reprinted, and remain in print to this day. The first, A *Ride to Khiva,* published in 1876, was the story of Burnaby's unofficial mission to the oasis town in central Asia which had recently been seized for the Tsar by General Kauffmann. The annexation of the ancient Khanate of Khiva was an episode in the imperial rivalry between Russia and Britain, which became known as 'the Great Game'. Russophobes, among whom Burnaby was prominent, were anxious to alert the British public to the threat they believed to be posed by Russia to Britain's position in India. Burnaby, like many officers on both sides, regarded a clash between the two great Asian Empires as an inevitability. In the winter of 1876-7, taking advantage of the generous leave allowed to officers of the Household Brigade, Burnaby set out again, this time accompanied by his manservant George Radford, to travel across the Turkish Empire from Constantinople to its eastern extremities, a journey lasting five months in very harsh conditions.

His central preoccupation was once again the perceived threat from Russia, this time to the integrity of Turkey and especially to its capital city, which guarded the passage from the Black Sea to the Mediterranean. Burnaby's account of the journey, *On Horseback through Asia Minor*, though hastily written, has been described by Peter Hopkirk, a recent travel writer and historian of 'the Great Game', as 'a marvellous book', to be bracketted with such classics as Kipling's *Kim* and Fitzroy Maclean's *Eastern Approaches*.[3]

The book proved very timely. In the spring of 1876 Gladstone had launched his famous campaign against 'the Bulgarian atrocities', accusing the Turks of inflicting massacres and cruelties upon the Christian peoples of the Balkans. This made it more difficult for Disraeli's Conservative government to render assistance to the Turks when, shortly after Burnaby's return to England, the Russians duly attacked Turkey. The debate raging in Britain over the future of the Turkish Empire, and especially Turkey in Europe, is known as 'the Eastern Question'.

Armed with unique first hand experience, Burnaby launched himself into this debate, calling for 50,000 troops to be sent to Constantinople and for subsidies to be offered to the Turkish government in order to improve the equipment of its army. His agenda went far beyond the defence of Constantinople: 'Russia could be driven out of Central Asia and forced to relinquish her hold on the Caucasus'.[4] Disraeli's government was not prepared to go that far but in January 1878 did send the fleet to Besika Bay, an implied threat which helped to persuade Tsar Alexander II to halt his armies at the gates of Constantinople and to revert to diplomacy.[5] It was during this period of heated debate in Britain that the word 'jingo' was coined to describe those pressing for war with Russia.[6] Burnaby was the arch-jingo. But not content to be a mere publicist, he managed to get himself attached to the Turkish army as a 'neutral' observer and hurried off to the scene of fierce fighting in the Balkan mountains. In total breach of protocol, he assumed command of a retreating Turkish battalion and led it to safety. He survived unscathed but his manservant was less fortunate, dying of typhus within hours of disembarking at Dover.

Burnaby's next adventure took him to Egypt and the Sudan. He joined General Baker who, in the serve of the Khedive of Egypt, was battling against the forces of the Mahdi for control of the Sudan. The Anglo-Egyptian forces suffered defeat at the Battle of El-Teb on 4 February 1882 but, strengthened by reinforcements, they turned the tables on the Mahdi's soldiers at the second Battle of El-Teb twenty-four days later. Burnaby was mentioned in despatches and received a wound in the arm, returning home an even more popular hero. Events in the Sudan unfolded like a Greek tragedy.

Figure 2. Colonel Fred Burnaby, parliamentary candidate for Birmingham. *R. Ward.*

In 1884 the Gladstone government despatched General Charles Gordon to the Sudan with orders to evacuate. Hesitating to withdraw, Gordon found himself besieged in Khartoum. A divided government delayed in sending a relief expedition which, when it was eventually sent under the command of General Sir Garnet Wolseley, tragically arrived two days late. Events were played out before a public avid for news. Burnaby's regiment was included in the relief expedition but it was hardly surprising that Burnaby himself, a major critic of the government's tardiness, was ordered to remain at home. Defying orders, Burnaby caught up with Wolseley at Wadi Halfa in December 1884 and was welcomed by his brother officers.

Thus it was that he was present at the Battle of Abu Klea on 17 January 1885 when Wolseley's advance guard was confronted by a strong force of the Mahdi's soldiers. In fierce hand-to-hand fighting, which cost the lives of eight British officers, sixty-five other ranks and over 600 Mahdists, Burnaby was wounded in the neck by a spear, surrounded and cut down. He was buried in the Sudan desert on the site of the battle.

'When word of Burnaby's death reached London', wrote Peter Hopkirk, 'the country was plunged into a frenzy of grief, for by this time he was almost a national institution'.[7] Not everyone, however, shared this grief. 'Burnaby seems to have come to his natural end', wrote John Bright, senior Member of Parliament for Birmingham, to Joseph Chamberlain. 'How strange that such a savage should be produced in what is called a Christian age and country'.[8] John Bright was the most distinguished representative of the anti-imperial tradition in British politics. He had resigned from Gladstone's government in 1882 over the issue of intervention in Egypt and was not a little disgusted with the junior MP for Birmingham, Chamberlain, for not following his example. Bright and his kind had often been the butt of scathing attacks by Burnaby and the 'jingoes' and the latter had carried that attack into Bright's 'home' territory of Birmingham.

In May 1878 Burnaby was adopted as Parliamentary candidate by the Birmingham Conservative Association. From that time until his death he remained committed to the Tory cause and was generally active in Birmingham and in neighbouring constituencies.

In political terms Birmingham Conservatives were as beleaguered as the Turks had been in Constantinople in 1877. It was the kind of challenge Burnaby could not resist while, for Conservatives, he embodied the characteristics which were so conspicuously lacking in the local party. In Birmingham Burnaby played out the last of his roles, as a politician.

The Birmingham Liberal Association, widely known as the 'caucus', was the most powerful organisation of its kind in the country. Formed in 1865, its objective was to mobilise Liberal opinion in Birmingham and to translate it into a monopoly of elected office. It reached the peak of its power in the 1870s and provided the electoral base for the famous mayoralty of Joseph Chamberlain from 1873-6. Chamberlain, though

Mr. S.—"Of course you will Vote for the Liberals?"

WORKING MAN.—"Not if I know it! I am going to Vote for BURNABY, CALTHORPE, and ENGLAND."

Figure 3. A cartoon of the period.
Birmingham Reference Library.

not one of its founders, became its presiding genius and fashioned it into an instrument of his overweening ambition. If the 'caucus' was democratic, in the sense that it sought to involve and represent the Liberal majority in the town, it was also hated for its intolerance of minorities and its monopolistic spirit.[9] 'We have had another Liberal triumph and carried the whole Board of Guardians by majorities of three to two,' crowed Chamberlain to his confidante, Jesse Collings, in 1876.

> *Think of that! A representative body of sixty, every manjack a Liberal and carried in the teeth of the Tories... . This is Liberal tyranny with a vengeance... . Council, School Board, Guardians are all ours. Never was there such a complete and absolute supremacy.*[10]

The situation in the Town Council was little different. In 1878 there was only one avowed Tory in a Council of sixty-four members. The 'caucus' was also accused of political jobbery – appointing supporters to posts in local government, schools, police, etc. in the manner of some American cities. Excluded from office and from public appointments, Birmingham Conservatives, when they dared show their faces, were subject to abuse and even physical violence.

'Few gentlemen of position will face the amount of "mud-throwing" they would have to endure', complained a local Conservative.[11] Sampson Samuel Lloyd, a leading banker and for years the town's leading Conservative, fought and lost Parliamentary elections in 1867 and 1868. In his diary he recorded that 'threats of personal violence were addressed to me which rendered it necessary on two or more occasions to wear a disguise on my way home'.[12] He complained also of damage done to his business interests. The Aston Riots of October 1884, when Radical thugs broke up a Tory rally in the Aston Lower Grounds, furnished an extreme example of 'caucus' violence.

Such militant partisanship made it extremely difficult for the Conservative party in Birmingham to function normally or effectively. In 1874 the Tories were unable to find a single candidate willing to stand in the general election and three Liberal candidates were returned unopposed.

From that low point a fight-back began. It was led locally by J B Stone,[13] and was encouraged by Conservative Central Office. In 1877 a Conservative 'caucus' was formed, very much on the Liberal model. In 1878 the annual meeting of the National Union of Conservative Associations was held in Birmingham and a rally at

Figure 4. The Burnaby Monument with St Philip's Cathedral, 1998. *R. Ward.*

Aston attracted a crowd of 30,000.[14] In his search for a Parliamentary candidate, Stone approached the Tory Chief Whip, Sir William Hart-Dyke, and the latter recommended Fred Burnaby. Renowned for his strength and physical courage and no mean platform performer, Burnaby seemed the ideal candidate for the 'Birmingham Balkans'. In return Birmingham furnished Burnaby with the kind of challenge he relished. 'I never fly at small game', he boasted, 'and besides if I were to win in Birmingham I should be offered a place in the cabinet'.[15]

For the next two years Burnaby cultivated his Birmingham constituency. One initiative of the Conservative Association was to found working men's clubs. Burnaby became President of one in Sparkbrook and became convinced of working class support for his party: 'with the help of the Conservative working man I shall yet carry Birmingham', he boasted.[16]

There was some substance to his hopes. His meetings were well attended, though often violent and rowdy. His coolness and physical courage were much admired. On two occasions, once in 1878 and again in 1884, the horses were unharnessed from his carriage and he was drawn through the principal streets of the town by working men. Burnaby was in fact first class political theatre. But could this be translated into solid electoral support?

As the election approached the Conservative Association prevailed on Augustus Calthorpe, heir to the valuable Calthorpe estate in Edgbaston, to join Burnaby in contesting Birmingham's three seats.

The election of 1880 was the last to be fought on a list system, each voter having two votes to distribute among the candidates. By putting up only two candidates the Conservatives hoped to win one of the seats, a hope that 'caucus' organisation set out to crush. It was a bitter and hard fought contest. For once it was Chamberlain who had cause to complain of 'the virulence with which the Tories have attacked me. No slander has been too gross, no calumny too improbable'.[17] Calthorpe, however, proved a weak candidate and wilted under the attacks of leading Liberals, many of whom were his father's tenants in Edgbaston. It was an unequal struggle. Philip Muntz, a popular local industrialist with a long record of service in Birmingham, topped the poll, followed by Bright and Chamberlain. Burnaby and Calthorpe came in fourth and fifth.[18]

The Tories were left to extract what comfort they could. They had polled nearly thirty thousand votes, against the Liberals 65,000.[18] They calculated that their increase on 1868 was eighty-nine per cent to the Liberals forty-five per cent.[19] There was scant comfort in these figures but the crucial fact was that the Tories had fought the election and were imbued with a new spirit. This was sufficient to encourage Lord Randolph Churchill, a man as thrusting and ambitious as Chamberlain, to take a growing interest in Birmingham.

In January 1884 he agreed to stand for Birmingham at the next general election. In April he and Burnaby shared a platform in the Birmingham Town Hall.[20] Both were present on the occasion of the Aston Riots in October 1884. Fate intervened.

The news of Burnaby's death was received in Birmingham with a grief which was not confined to Conservative circles. In contrast to John Bright's uncharitable comments, Chamberlain paid Burnaby a generous tribute:

> *We all share the deep regret which is felt in Birmingham at the death in the moment of victory of Colonel Burnaby... . In the presence of such a calamity political controversies are hushed, and we have only to deplore the loss of as brave a soldier as ever wore the British uniform.*[21]

Other evidence suggests that Burnaby and Chamberlain had met together privately and enjoyed each other's company.[22] Is it too fanciful to suppose that some of Burnaby's enthusiasm for Empire left its mark on Chamberlain? A sense of the important role Burnaby played in reviving the spirit of Conservatism in Birmingham led the editor of the Birmingham Daily Gazette, B H Grindley, to launch an appeal for funds for a memorial to Burnaby.

On 13 November 1885 the obelisk was unveiled by Lord Charles Beresford, another popular military figure, who afterwards addressed a public meeting in the Town Hall, 'which was crowded in every part'.[23] Burnaby – Khiva – Abu Klea: this was all that was needed to identify this extraordinary figure of the age of imperialism.

Notes and References

1. There have been two biographies of Burnaby: T Wright, *The Life of Colonel Fred Burnaby* (1908) and M Alexander, *The True Blue* (1957). There is also biographical material in an introduction to *A Ride to Khiva* (1972) by D G Williams and in the preface to the 1997 edition by Peter Hopkirk.
2. He was also the subject of a cartoon in the famous Spy series (Leslie Ward) labelled simply 'Fred', *Vanity Fair*, 2 December 1876.
3. Preface to Burnaby, F *On Horseback through Asia Minor* (1996).
4. *Ibid*, p328.
5. The issues were resolved at the Congress of Berlin (June – July 1878). The Congress is usually considered a triumph for Disraeli, created the Early of Beaconsfield in 1876.
6. From a popular song, in a version circulating in Birmingham:
   We don't want to fight, yet by jingo when we do we've got the ships, we've got the men, and got the money too. We've fought the Bear before and the Turks have proved so true

The Russians shan't have Constantinople.

7. Epilogue to *On Horseback.*

8. Bright to Chamberlain, 27 January 1885. Joseph Chamberlain Papers 5/16/50.

9. For a favourable account of the 'caucus', see A Briggs, *History of Birmingham* Vol. 2 (1952), chapter 6.

10. Joseph Chamberlain to Jesse Collings, 10 April 1876, JCP 5/16/50.

11. Letter to *Birmingham Daily Gazette* (BDG), 15 December 1884.

12. Lloyd, S S Autobiographical Memoir (MSS), 6.

13. Later Stone, Sir J.P. MP for East Birmingham.

14. BDG, 25 October 1879.

15. Wright, T *Life of Burnaby*, 153.

16. *Ibid.*

17. Garvin, J L *Life of Joseph Chamberlain* Vol. 1 (1932), p278.

18. Result: Muntz 22,803, Burnaby 15,716, Bright 21,986, Calthorpe 14,270, Chamberlain 19,746

19. *Birmingham Conservative Association Annual Report*, 1884.

20. BDG, 16 April 1884.

21. Quoted in Wright, T *Life of Burnaby,* 308.

22. *Ibid*, 244.

23. *Birmingham Conservative Association Annual Report*, 1885.

10. HAZELWOOD AND THE HILLS: AN EXPERIMENT IN EDUCATION

by Chris Upton

BIRMINGHAM HAS BEEN AT the cutting edge of many educational reforms over the years. The campaign for free elementary schooling in the nineteenth century began in Birmingham, as did the 'open classroom', the numeracy hour and the University of the First Age in the twentieth. But perhaps the most radical experiment of them all has been almost entirely forgotten, even though at the time it attracted interest (and pupils) from as far afield as Scandinavia and Greece, Argentina and the Caribbean. One edition of *Encyclopaedia Britannica* placed it alongside the work of Dr Arnold of Rugby.[1] It's high time we remembered it.

The story begins in 1803, with the purchase of a boys' school to the south of Birmingham called 'Hill Top' by Thomas Wright Hill.[2] The name alone might have attracted his attention, but like any private establishment it was there to be fashioned into the kind of education one thought suitable for the new age. Thomas Hill might be a new name to many, but by his sons you will know him. One son, Matthew Davenport, became the Recorder of Birmingham and Member of Parliament for Hull,[3] whilst another, Rowland Hill (Figure 1), created the Penny Post.[4] Both men initially studied and later taught at their father's school.

Thomas Hill's pioneering work began at a school in Lionel Street in the town centre, moving to Hill Top in 1803 and then to a new school called Hazelwood on the Hagley Road in 1819. But before we look at this, we need to remind ourselves of the state of English education in the early nineteenth century. The kind of schooling on offer, pioneered by the great public schools of Eton and Harrow, and mimicked by the

Figure 1. Rowland Hill 1795-1879.
Birmingham Reference Library.

grammar schools, was stodgily traditional. The diet of Latin and Greek was not so different to what had been offered in Shakespeare's day, reinforced by liberal (or not so liberal) use of the cane. The philosopher, Jeremy Bentham, writing for the Hazelwood school magazine in 1823, brought to the pupils' attention the recent retirement of an 'active schoolmasteri' in Spain. During his career, Bentham calculated, the master had administered 911,500 canings and 124,000 floggings![5] Across Europe, and especially across England, it was as if the Enlightenment and the Industrial Revolution had never happened.

In Birmingham, however, things were slightly different. The *ex-officio* home of the Lunar Society and the birthplace of the industrial world was not quite so rooted in tradition. It was with an awareness of the changing needs of society that Thomas Wright and particularly his son, Rowland, addressed the issue of education. Certainly the

Figure 2. Hazelwood School Yard from a sketch by the late Samuel Lines. *Birmingham Reference Library.*

Figure 3. Hazelwood School, Hagley Road. *Birmingham Reference Library.*

curriculum followed at Hazelwood could not be more different. Latin and Greek were there, for sure, but so were modern languages: French, Italian, German and Spanish. However, it was not only their presence, but also the way they were taught, that was unique. The Hills implemented the 'direct method' of language learning, as Rowland made clear in 1833:

> *We think that French and indeed all the living languages should be acquired, as nearly as our means allow, in the same manner as a child learns its mother tongue.*[6]

Better still, a native French teacher was employed to help the process along. More curiously, geography was taught in French in the top class.

Elsewhere too the Hagley Road curriculum offered a breadth of subjects not often seen in England before the twentieth century: geography, surveying, mechanics, science, metalwork, drama, music and art. Rowland Hill, in the scheme quoted above, gives an example of the kind of reading matter recommended for the pupil's 'private study':

> *Results of Machinery. School Bible. Mutiny on the Bounty. Pleasures and Advantages of Science. Life of Ferguson. Entertaining Knowledge (Vol. VIII: Insect Architecture). Travels at Home (Vol. Ill: Asia). White's Natural History of Selborne. Coriolanus. Julius Caesar.*[7]

The amount of science in the Hazelwood timetable (amounting to around thirteen hours a week) was remarkable, and clearly influenced by Thomas Hill's own enthusiasm for it. He was, after all, a devoted follower of Joseph Priestley.

To support this varied curriculum Hazelwood had its own science lab (one of the first in the country), as well as workshops and tool-shed, observatory, swimming pool and music room, all specifically designed by Rowland Hill. (Hill also designed the unique central-heating system in the school.) In addition, the boys kept guinea pigs and rabbits, furnished a school museum and had their own printing press (lent to them by the Hills) for publishing the school magazine. They even designed an innovatory piece of machinery which peeled the potatoes in the school kitchen. The surviving school magazines show that the boys could be performing extracts from Shakespeare or Latin plays by Plautus on one day, and conducting electrical experiments with an egg on the next. They were even known to volunteer for extra Greek lessons! Nor were the pupils only active in the classroom and the laboratory. Parties of boys could be seen taking measurements in the Bull Ring, and an excursion party, calling themselves 'the Franks' went on expeditions across the West Midlands. Generally they walked![8]

Yet all this was not the most innovatory side of life at Hazelwood. What attracted even more attention was the way the school was run. Here there was no canewielding autocracy – corporal punishment was banned – but a government shared between teachers and pupils. The boys themselves elected a committee which enacted laws and fixed the penalties for offences. Those who broke the rules were tried before a jury of their peers – choosing their own advocate if necessary – and they received a punishment decided by a school judge. Such responsibilities could be arduous: in November 1822, for example, the jury was sitting from before breakfast until nine o'clock in the evening over a particularly serious offence. The school magazine noted that they did not eat during this time. The pupils themselves were divided into 'circles' of ten boys each, with a member of the committee (called a 'guardian') at the head of each. It was the guardian's duty to offer advice and counselling, and to levy fines when the school laws had been breached. The Reform movement was still some way off in England at large, but there were unmistakably democratic tendencies in the Hazelwood regime.

It would be wrong to single out the system of fines and punishment at Hazelwood without counterbalancing it with reference to the rewards. Hazelwood had its own currency of 'marks',

Figure 4. Hazelwood School, Hagley Road. *Birmingham Reference Library.*

metal tokens which could be earned by excellence in the classroom or by additional work and duties. Such coinage could be exchanged for extra holidays, or lost through misdemeanours.

The benefits of success and the costs of mischief were felt immediately in the pocket. Frederick Harrold, on leaving the school in 1822 left 5,000 penal marks (as a kind of posthumous bequest) to various chosen individuals.[9] It was all perfectly legal. After devaluation in May 1824, incidentally, 5,000 marks were worth just over four shillings (20p).

Inevitably this extraordinary system attracted much comment and interest from the outside world. We have mentioned the favourable impression it made on one of the country's most influential philosophers, Jeremy Bentham. The author, Thomas de Quincey, reviewed Rowland Hill's book with obvious enthusiasm, and the school was visited by a procession of great names (rather too many, as far as the owners were concerned). The French educationalist (and secretary to Robbespierre), Marc Jullien, paid a visit in September 1822, followed by Robert Owen of New Lanark in May 1824. Thomas Malthus was there too, as well as William Wilberforce, Nassau Senior (the poor law reformer), Charles Babbage (the 'father' of computers) and the Marquess of Landsdowne. Favourable reviews in the journals similarly flowed in, from the London Magazine, the Edinburgh Review, the Guardian and the National Register, to name just a few. One writer in the Westminster Review went as far as to say:

On this admirable system of education the brightest hopes of the human race may anchor. The system has commenced its career; it must go on; it will become universal... [10]

Inevitably such glowing tributes reached ears far beyond English shores. There was a visit from the Libyan ambassador in September 1822 and interested enquiries from across Europe and the Americas, including a request for Rowland's and Matthew's book, Public Education, from Thomas Jefferson. Boys were sent to Hazelwood from Greece, France, Portugal and Mexico, and the trio of pupils who arrived from Buenos Aires in October 1824 included the son of the former Argentinian president, Senor Rodrigues. A school upon similar principles, and named 'Hillska Skolan' after the Hills, was set up near Stockholm in 1830. [11] Collections were also made at the school to support the Greek independence movement. All this international activity on the Hagley Road over 150 years ago!

By the mid-1820s Hazelwood was at the height of its fame and attracting considerably more pupils (about 150) than King Edward's. But its fall was equally swift. In 1827 the school was transferred to a sister institution at Bruce Castle in Tottenham. But in middle-class London the Hills were battling with parents who were considerably less enlightened in their educational horizons. Science had to be abandoned in favour of a more traditional diet and, when Rowland's health failed in 1833, the school was closed for good. Whatever the *Westminster Review* believed, it is clear that it was the commitment and energy (and money) which the Hill family brought to the project that drove it forward. Once recovered, Rowland Hill took his energies elsewhere.

Ultimately, of course, the reputation of a school stands or fails on

Figure 5. Hazelwood School, 1959. *Birmingham Reference Library.*

the achievement of its scholars, and it's interesting to see that many of Hazelwood's successful alumni found careers in the sciences, industry and politics. John Gent Bowman became the first chairman of BSA and chairman of the Midland Bank; William Scholefield was Birmingham's first mayor and later a Member of Parliament; Arthur Follett Osier (who donated to the school a working model of a Trevithick steam engine) became a Birmingham glass manufacturer, whose glass fountain graced the Crystal Palace; Sir William Bowman is known for his pioneering work in anatomy. And of course there were the younger Hills themselves.

The exact location of the school has caused some confusion over the years and a number of historians wrongly link it to King Edward's (Five Ways). It was, in fact, much further along the Hagley Road, on the south side, opposite to the entrance to Portland Road.

Early trade directories suggest that after the school closed, the building was owned by Abraham Follett Osier, the industrialist and an ex-pupil of Hazelwood. His address is listed as 'Hazelwood' in the 1850s and 1860s. Hazelwood was demolished in the late 1950s and an office block now occupies the site.[12]

As for the long-term effect of Hazelwood, this is more difficult to assess. We can hardly attribute to an institution which lasted only fourteen years too great an influence, but at a time when England in general was beginning to question the way her parliamentary democracy was being run, and to understand the relationship between society and its schools, Hazelwood and its former pupils undoubtedly contributed to the debate. Indeed, one former scholar, William Sargant, became a key member of the Birmingham-based National Education League, which campaigned for (and finally achieved) elementary schooling for all in the 1860s.

Undoubtedly the achievements and vision of Hill Top and Hazelwood are something of which Birmingham ought to be proud.

Notes and References

1. The claim is made in the ninth edition of *Encyclopaedia Britannica*, 1875 in the entry under Rowland Hill.

2. Edwards Eleizer, Sir Rowland Hill, London, 1879, pp 25-6. Hill-Top stood on the raised ground at the corner of Gough Street and Blucher Street. According to Edwards the Jewish synagogue now occupies part of the garden of the house.

3. Davenport Hill Rosamond & Florence, *The Recorder of Birmingham. A Memoir of Matthew Davenport Hill*, London, 1878.

4. There are a number of biographies of Rowland, most of them inevitably concentrating on his work for the post office. The most recent study, Hey Colin G, *Rowland Hill. Victorian Genius and Benefactor*, London, 1989, gives due and full consideration to his educational work.

5. The *Hazelwood Magazine*, May 1823, p 3.

6. Rowland Hill, *Sketch of the System of Education, Moral and Intellectual in Practice at the Schools of Bruce Castle, Tottenham, and Hazelwood, near Birmingham*, Birmingham & London, 1833, p 24. See also Hill Rowland & Matthew, *Public Education. Plans for the Governance and Liberal Instruction of Boys in Large Numbers, as Practised at Hazelwood School*, London, 1825.

7. *Ibid.*, pp 15-16.

8. This brief account of life at Hazelwood, in all its rich variety, is taken from numerous references in the school magazine. The *Hazelwood Magazine* ran from September 1822 to December 1830 and a full set can be found in Local Studies & History in Birmingham Central Library, SC 5.

9. Drafted as Mr F Harrold's Will in *The Hazelwood Magazine*, September 1822, pp 2-5.

10. Quoted in Hey CG, pp 5-6.

11. Ericsson H, *Hillska Skolan a Barnangen 1830-1846*, Stockholm, 1885. A copy can be found in the Local Studies pamphlet collection. An account of the opening ceremony and the speech by the delightfully named Count Frolick is printed in *The Hazelwood Magazine*, September-October 1830.

12. The house called Hazelwood Lodge on the Ordnance Survey 1:500 map of 1887 does survive, though its connection with the school is as yet unknown.

11. INTRODUCING WALLER JEFFS

by Christopher Dingley

A CARTOON IN THE FILM trade paper *The Bioscope*, dating from 1911, presents a man of middle years wearing evening dress (with buttonhole), wire-framed spectacles and a bushy moustache waxed into tips. Benign, a touch remote, he might pass for a professor of philosophy, or perhaps a crystal ball gazer. From one hand he scatters papers – 'Amusement,' 'Instruction,' 'Travel' – while in the other he holds a baton which points at Birmingham Town Hall, far below. His name is Waller Jeffs, and he is riding a magic carpet.[1]

Walter who? Once upon a time in Birmingham Osmund Waller Jeffs needed no introduction. Iris Barry, first curator of film at New York's Museum of Modern Art, remembered being taken as a child to

> *a delectable place called Waller Jeffs' Pictures... we walked a mile into town and went into the darkness to wonder and cry 'Ooh' at jigging photographs... that not only showed you things, but showed them moving.*[2]

Michael Balcon of Ealing comedy fame called Jeffs 'the man responsible for stimulating my own early interest in the cinema.'[3] Mrs E Johnson of Rednal, simply someone who happened to write to the papers on the matter, recalled being petrified by sudden inexplicable screen horses: 'my mother probably wished she hadn't taken me because I asked so many questions.'[4] It seems Jeffs never had children but, like Mr Chips, could have claimed untold numbers.

Between the dawn of cinema as a novelty in the 1890s and its consolidation as an industry in the 1910s came an age of travelling showmen; men like Jeffs who, with his annual seasons at Curzon Hall between 1901 and 1912, introduced a generation of Birmingham folk to film.[5] Under his banner of New Century Pictures he promised 'the world from pole to pole' but reached still further, flying his audience to the moon with Georges Melies and, almost as astonishingly, taking them down the Bristol Road by tram.[6] Towards the end of his pioneer days, it was said

> *Mr Jeffs has with the deft touch of a magician's wand given us the*

wonders of a universe, the world's beauty spots. He has illustrated to us the miracles of science, historical incidents, and subjects embracing drama, art, fun and humour – endless and bewildering in their variety and beauty.[7]

A hundred years on, the people he dazzled with shadows are shadows themselves. Leaving behind the century we shared, it seems high time we reacquainted ourselves with this magician, the father of Birmingham film.

Curzon Hall, near the top end of Suffolk Street, was a great barn of a building housing some three thousand spectators (as many as five thousand for Jeffs' annual charity children's matinees).[8] Built in 1865 for the Birmingham Dog Show, it soon became home also to such pre–cinematic screen spectacles as panoramas and magic lanternshows. A Christmastide attraction over many years was Harry H Hamilton's Excursions, a rolling display of painted scenic cloths which passed across an illuminated twenty by twelve foot screen, conducted by the comments of a guide or 'cicerone', embellished by music, lighting and sound effects.[9] Jeffs was a journalist turned lecturer turned showman who by century's end was an adept in this disappearing Victorian world of Pleasure Travel. Film promised new worlds, and after acquiring his first cinematograph around 1898 he started showing moving pictures alongside his lanternslides.

It was as touring manager for the Thomas–Edison Animated Photo Company that Jeffs opened his first Curzon Hall film season on 6 May 1901.[10] Britain was fighting the Boers in Africa and the Boxers in China, and his programme capitalised on the war mood with what purported to be actual campaign footage 'taken by the latest and most wonderful invention the telephoto lens... reproducing the living incidents of actual warfare at your own doors.'[11] A particular hit later that season was a work of admitted fiction, James

Figure 1. The popular Birmingham weekly newspaper *The Owl* which advertised and reviewed many of Jeff's presentations.
Birmingham Reference Library.

Williamson's classic of early British cinema, *Attack on a China mission*; 'and what a cheer the audience gave,' it was reported, when the navy's bluejackets arrived at the rescue.[12] Closer to home, yet no less foreign to local eyes, was a film about Birmingham. *Return of the gallant Warwicks*, shot the week before, offered exclusive pictures of a parade through the city by the Birmingham Volunteer Brigade of the Royal Warwickshire Regiment, just back from Africa. The crowded streets were captured, with the Lord Mayor's blessing, from the Town Hall roof.

Otherwise, in a programme

CURZON HALL

New Century Picture Palace.

MR. JEFFS' NEW PICTURES.

THE NAVAL DISASTER OFF THE NEEDLES.

The Wrecked Cruiser, "Gladiator," and the Damaged Liner, "St. Paul."

Mr. Jeffs' New Pathetic Story Picture, "FOR THE CHILDREN'S SAKE."

Every Day at 3. **TWICE DAILY** Every Night at 8.

Prices, Reserved Seats, 2s. 6d., 2s., 1s. 6d.
Amission, 1s., 6d., 3d.

Figure 2. Advertisement for *The Naval Disaster off the Needles*, 1908. *Birmingham Reference Library.*

lasting more than two hours, twice daily, and boasting 'five miles of film,'[13] pictures ranged from Queen Victoria's funeral to 'the funniosities of a couple in the enjoyment of a feast of kissing' (possibly Edison's *May Irwin–John C Rice Kiss* of 1896).[14] 'As well as the longest, the collection of films is undoubtedly the best that the city has seen,' it was said.[15] Technical quality, then a common concern, was praised for the 'absence of shadow, flicker and flaws.'[16] A cicerone, most likely Jeffs himself, performed, as did the Edgbaston Military Band, a choir, and a ventriloquist.

The success of the *Gallant Warwicks* film and an opportune spell of fine mid–May weather encouraged Jeffs to seek out fresh visions of Birmingham. These included – in homage, one hopes, to the Lumiere Brothers' first film – *Workpeople leaving factories*, a series showing the five o'clock flight from Kynoch's, Nettlefold's, Tangye's, the Patent Nut and Bolt Co, and others; a reviewer found it 'amusing to see the hustling there is to catch the camera's eye.'[17] Lovers of early cinema will be gladdened to learn also that Jeffs went on a phantom ride that first spring *The phantom tram ride*, shot from the top of a new electric tramcar heading down the Bristol Road towards town. Other local scenes were taken in Chamberlain Square, Old Square, and at an Aston Villa–Sheffield United cup-tie. 'Come and see yourselves on the screen' urged Jeffs[18] and few seemed inclined to resist.

Extended several times before finally having to close on 13 July,

Curzon Hall. Mr. Waller Jeff's entrancing entertainment at Curzon Hall should not be missed by young or old. It is really delightful. The pictures are so perfect, so realistic. The tour through "Bonnie Scotland" in itself merits all the praise we could bestow. Those who haven't seen "the land of the Mountain and the Flood," have only to see the pictures and long to see the original, while those who know Scotland will be more than delighted as familiar scenes are brought again to mind. Then then are the humourous pictures at which everyone laughs a really hearty and healthy laugh. Not least clever and interesting is the exhibition of direct colour protographs, examples of what can be done by the latest scientific processes.

Figure 3. A typical review of Jeff's presentation, 1908. *Birmingham Reference Library.*

Jeffs' May 1901 season must be considered a landmark as significant in its way as Birmingham's first sight of film in 1896. A hundred and twenty performances had attracted three hundred thousand people: a third of Birmingham, in ten weeks. 'We shall return', said Jeffs.[19]

He had encountered little real competition, nor would do for several years. Cinema was a vagrant art, lacking as yet the confidence of capital and thus with no home of its own. Films were still being shown in music halls, though often as chasers to clear the house ahead of the National Anthem; the Birmingham Hippodrome showed them as such from 1902. Films were also fairground attractions; as early as 1897 Birmingham's Onion Fair was playing host to such arcane delights as Wadbrook's Ghost and Electrical Cinematographe and Chittock's Dog and Monkey Circus and Cinematographe.[20] Finally there was the raw cinema of the penny gaffs or shopshows, primitive gone–tomorrow displays crammed into vacant commercial premises, unknown numbers of which came and went without troubling posterity. We are fortunate to have this terse account of one, somewhere in Digbeth, circa 1908:

The shop is fourteen feet wide by twenty feet long; only one door, 2ft 6in wide, which opens inward to shop. Woman sat in chair by door taking admission money – one penny each; about sixty persons admitted each time; seating, boards on ginger beer boxes; door closed when full. Windows obscured with brown paper; lantern placed on wood box on show board of window, and wall of shop whitewashed forms screen; picture about six feet by nine. Heads of those sitting in front row on picture screen.[21]

Jeffs brought films in from the margins; his shows declared and inspired faith. 'Perhaps you may be dubious as to whether animated photographs can give you a whole evening's entertainment,' a critic remarked, 'but one visit to Curzon Hall makes you wonder why you thought so.'[22] For the first time of any consequence Birmingham audiences were being given film not as novelty, sideshow or added attraction, but the main event.

Yet we should note that the 1901 shows were a step away, not a break from the past; a bloodless coup, perhaps, with much of the old guard retained. Jeffs and his audience were alike children of the pre-cinema, with a shared understanding of its modes and moods – the cicerone, the pleasure travel, the didactic, improving air. He simply made the animated rather than the non-animated the dominant element in a continuing tradition of screen spectacle. And by conserving the old while making soothing noises about the new, he was able to bring with him on his journey a hitherto filmshy middle class audience who came to regard him as someone they could do business with. Dreams came not a penny each at Curzon Hall but from sixpence up to three shillings, so master and servant could dream the same dreams without having to rub shoulders. To flourish, film needed both, and both took their appointed places at Waller Jeffs Pictures.

The only note of disappointment recorded that first season arose when a film of the *university degree day procession* from Edmund Street to the Town Hall, filmed on the Saturday, was not ready as promised by the Monday evening.[23] It was a lesson Jeffs took to heart, with regard both to the appetite for such local material and the need to deliver it promptly. Before long it would be said 'if Mr Jeffs continues on his present most enterprising lines, we shall expect him to snapshot the audience as they enter the hall, develop the film during the performance and show them themselves on the screen after half-time.'[24] The notion, fostered by Jeffs, that spectators might indeed see their shadowselves on screen, was backed up by regular press reports of such recognitions.[25] While we may sometimes doubt their literal truth, these reports surely reflected a wider, cultural truth: Birmingham was for the first time recognising itself on film. For a new century a new witness, a new means of representation was among us, touching our streets, our occasions, and even our faces.

Of the famous or then famous faces filmed by Jeffs, three stand out today – Edward VII, Joseph Chamberlain and Buffalo Bill. The King came to Birmingham in July 1909 to open the new University buildings at Edgbaston, and *The Royal Visit – how Birmingham welcomed the King* included 'illustrations of the triumphant arches, their Majesties' arrival at the Council House, Mrs Chamberlain presenting a bouquet to the Queen, and the scenes of enthusiasm manifested during the journey to the University.'[26]

Chamberlain was an early friend of cinema in Birmingham. It was a strategy of Jeffs on arriving in a new town to seek the support of local dignitaries such as 'lord mayors, chief constables, a duke and a duchess, a peer, bishops, knights, magistrates and clergy.'[27] In Birmingham he surpassed himself by bagging its first citizen and the then Colonial Secretary, under whose 'Distinguished Patronage' his May 1901 season opened.[28] Chamberlain subsequently agreed to be filmed at a number of local events, beginning with that keenly-awaited Degree Day Procession. In 1902 he was shown making a speech at his Highbury home during a Presentation of medals to the St John's Ambulance Brigade, though the sight of the great man's silent posturings provoked hilarity at Curzon Hall: 'someone was heard to appeal to Mr Chamberlain to 'Speak up!' while another, noting the fact that by the clapping of hands a telling point in the speech had touched those who listened, shouted out with considerable feeling, 'Hear, hear!'[29] He was last filmed for Jeffs outside the Council House in July 1906 during his seventieth birthday celebrations, described as 'the greatest birthday party the world has ever seen.[30] The resulting film *The Chamberlain Procession* soon took on a tragic significance; within days its central figure had suffered the stroke which forced him from public life.

William 'Buffalo Bill' Cody's surprising claim on Birmingham cinema came in June 1903 when he paraded through the city centre with his company, the Wild West and Congress of Rough Riders of the World, during a fortnight's engagement at Perry Barr. Real cowboys and Indians rode the streets that day, with other startling sights, and at their head, drawn in a barouche by two milk–white steeds, the legendary western showman himself, white–haired but clear–eyed, smiling his 'frank, manly smile.'[31] This time observers were aware they were witnessing the end of an era: 'the Indians are disappearing, the buffalo are gone,' wrote one, 'and this is the farewell of Colonel W F Cody'.[32] One imagines the Curzon Hall cicerone struck a similarly elegiac note as *Buffalo Bill's Parade*, filmed in its entirety, was passing ghostly across the screen.

Jeffs produced many topicals during his years in Birmingham (and produced has to be the word – we have no way of knowing how many of his films he took himself, or how many he commissioned others to take for him).[33] Most were tales of the expected, brief accounts of ceremonial or other pre–arranged spectacle whether civic, military or sporting. Subjects included *Band of Hope procession to Aston Park* (1903), *Scenes at the military gymkhana at Moseley* (1904), *Parade of Corporation horses* (1905), *Funeral of a Birmingham military veteran* (1906), *Warwickshire Yeomanry in camp* (1907), *Run from Curzon Hall to Wolverhampton* (1908), *Inspection of Boy Scouts by Baden–Powell at Warley Woods* (1909) and *Turn–out and drill by the Birmingham Fire Brigade* (1911). Some of these titles have not appeared in print since the films themselves first saw the light; but Birmingham's filmography begins here, with these and many more long–lost images.[34]

Iris Barry retained intense if somewhat vague impressions of her first films at Curzon Hall: 'express trains with huge cow–catchers in front of them, rushing and snorting towards one... Indians on piebald ponies who rode, all feathers and eyes, down through the prairies, though I forget who they were chasing.' One detail remained precise, however, and that was the name of the enterprise: *Waller Jeffs Pictures.*'[35] Jeffs took late to showbusiness, but in his self–promotion revealed himself a born showman. In a full–page advertisement carried by the Birmingham weekly *The Owl* in 1907 it is his name in the biggest letters and his name above the title. His portrait, too, is reproduced.[36] Today this cult of the exhibitor strikes us as strange; how could such prominence be justified?

Cinema in 1901 lacked much we would regard as essential. It was a cinema without stars or feature films, without established systems of publicity, distribution or regulation. It was a cinema without sound; even, as we have seen, a cinema without cinemas. Into this open city stepped the showman: he claimed it and named it. Visitors to Curzon Hall literally entered under Jeffs' name, picked out over the entrance arch, illuminated at night by naphtha flares, later limelight.[37] That name alone stood, it was said, as 'passport and surety' for whatever lay within.[38] In a cinema of such uncharacteristic self–effacement, the public had no–one else to turn to, nothing else to trust. Jeffs' face was the public image, his name the trademark, his pledges 'to cause a smile, and perchance a tear, but ne'er a blush'[39] the contract. And his pictures – *Waller Jeffs' Pictures* – were just that, bought outright by him at fourpence a foot.

Jeffs intervened in his filmshows to a degree quite unknown to later exhibitors. In an evening he might screen a dozen pictures, maybe a score, some no longer than today's trailers. In January 1906, titles on offer included *Two little waifs, Father's day out, The Babes in the wood, The Prince of India, Winter sports, Dream of Dickens, Grandpapa and the butterfly, A trip up the Nile, Bringing home the goose,*

Visit to the circus and Stolen by gypsies.[40] Added to which would be band numbers, lanternslide interludes and an assortment of turns which by 1911 was described (optimistically) as 'difficult to beat in any variety hall in the provinces.'[41] If such various items were, as once reported, 'skillfully woven together,'[42] then it was to Jeffs' credit as the weaver, arranging his reels and jigs into running orders which made some kind of narrative, emotional or at least business sense. A dramatic climax might be followed by an illustrated song, sung live by a soprano, the words thrown up on screen; after breath held, a rousing chorus. Unavoidable breaks while films were changed served sometimes to heighten suspense, sometimes to boost chocolate sales. It was said that at Curzon Hall the camera was always in service of the performance, meaning not that the films were subordinate so much as constituent, parts of a whole, like brief passages in a wide–ranging address.[43]

And a Jeff's show was a performance, with a live element which reached deep into the films themselves. Jeffs often played host; though he employed other cicerones, he remained a master of that dying art, as late as 1911 delivering a series of Ten-Minute Travel Talks by lanternlight. Stood by the side of the screen, mixing erudition and badinage, riding and guiding the crowd's moodswings, the cicerone brought narration and commentary, a measure of order and meaning to what might otherwise have been merely a riot of images. With his baton he provided emphasis and focus at a time when close–ups were infrequent, and audiences less cineliterate. The baton served also as a symbol of his power: reaching sometimes prodigious lengths (the Hamilton's Excursions man was said to wield one in white, seven feet long) and commonly compared to a magician's wand, it seemed to conjure visions from nowhere. Young Michael Balcon never forgot Jeffs declaring, in standard ciceronese, 'We are now in China.'[44] We can only imagine the air of hey–presto he imparted to that particular white rabbit.

The cicerone was just part of the

Figure 4. Curzon Hall at the top of Suffolk Street. *V. Price.*

soundworld the showman created for his pictures. Music was of course also a vital ingredient, provided at Curzon Hall not by the tinkling piano of fleapit mythology but a 'full band and choir' under the accomplished direction of Jeffs' 'chef d'orchestre' Joseph Engleman, who often used his own compositions as accompaniment.[45] Sometimes members of the company would supply voices for the mute figures onscreen, especially in the hullabaloo of action scenes. Sound effects too were hard to ignore: 'our horses did gallop, and no mistake,' Jeffs admitted. 'It never rained but it poured... and as for gunfire, what barrage could be worse, or better as the case may be, than two excited kiddies flogging a piece of linoleum with sticks for all they were worth?'[46]

For his more elaborate films Jeffs prepared a 'working plot' including all these elements. A fragment of one such, for *A Voyage across the Atlantic* in 1902, indicates basic musical cues ('A Life on the Ocean Waves'), sound effects (a steam whistle), and voices off ('Man overboard – man the boats!'). The cicerone is advised to 'observe the captain has got his sea legs on!'[47] Rarely, it seems, was silence less silent than in these early days of live cinema.

The simple term showman encompassed a complex of responsibilities and interventions – creative, performative, commercial, clerical. Only recently has his role been reappraised as that of

Figure 5. Poster advertising films at Curzon Hall, 1906. *V. Price.*

'the author of the show.'[48] Perhaps to Birmingham audiences Jeffs was something more; in his years of unchallenged ascendancy, this man who arrived out of the blue each year with his cinematograph and calico screen, carrying the world in his luggage, must have appeared the very incarnation of cinema.

Asked in 1907 for his thoughts on the future of film, Jeffs anticipated 'development and competition, with a tendency towards combination.'[49] That year brought him his first serious rival, the Kings Hall in Corporation Street, a converted chapel advertised as 'the only picture hall in the city open all the year round,'[50] and promising patrons, in a low but telling blow, 'no tedious lecturing.'[51]

Birmingham's first wave of purpose–built cinemas was launched in 1910 in the wake of the *Cinematograph Act* which, requiring all film exhibition to be licensed, drove the shopshows off the streets. The New Street Picture House, opened in October by the London combine Provincial Cinematograph Theatres was proclaimed one of the city's most handsome buildings, its seats 'possibly the most luxurious ever used in any theatres.'[52] By early 1912, with forty–three licences already granted under the Act, Jeffs was struggling for air space.[53] His form of presentation, of live, lecturer–driven cinema, had all but had its day. Audiences no longer needed films telling to them in this way, partly because of the efforts of Jeffs and his fellows, partly because film itself was absorbing the cicerone's function (with close-ups, continuity editing, intertitles), and partly – perhaps fundamentally – because people went to the pictures seeking escape not improvement. Nor was it enough to present cinema as something seasonal; it was becoming a pastime as routine in its way as the park or the pub. Like other pioneers Jeffs had awakened a demand he could not supply. He had opened a door, and held it open; other, less engaging individuals pushed past, as they had to.

In March 1912 *The Bioscope*, the paper which months earlier had cartooned him in his element, reported his fall to earth, to the tune of £1800. At a time when a moneystorm was breaking over the industry, he could guarantee his creditors just a shilling in the pound.[54] Leaving for London, he took a way of showing and enjoying film with him. Two years later his old dreamhouse became the city's chief recruiting office; the entrance which once had led to pretend African battlefields now led, for real, to the Somme.

Jeffs' story has a happy ending. Though no longer his own boss, he returned to the Midlands for a lengthy career in cinema management, firstly at the Harborne Picture House in Serpentine Road and, from 1921

Figure 6. The Scala Cinema, Smallbrook Street which opened in 1914. *V. Price.*

Figure 7. The Harborne Picture Palace, Serpentine Road. Walter Jeffs was manager in 1920. *V. Price.*

until his death, the Picture House at Stratford-upon-Avon.[55] He died in 1941, aged eighty, and is buried modestly at Brandwood End. His headstone, in the form of an open book, carries an inscription from *As you like it*: 'I will chide no breather in the world, except myself, 'gainst whom I know most fault.' There is mention too of his wife Marion, dead many years earlier, and his father, identified as a surgeon of St John's Wood, even down to the letters after his name. The stone tells nothing of Jeffs' own life's work.

If his life ever was an open book, it comes down to us with many leaves missing; there are gaps in his CV you could ride a magic carpet through. His first forty years, for instance, are obscured and likely to remain so. Then there are unanswered questions such as where, if anywhere, did he call home during his travelling years? And what was the true nature and extent of his dealings in the film world? Derby claims him as its own 'pioneer of film presentation' for shows he gave there while pioneering also in Birmingham.[56] How many other English towns would we need to trawl before exhausting all traces of his influence? Ultimately there is the question of Jeffs himself, 'serene, smiling, immaculate', 'honourable and honoured', yet at this distance, behind his cloak of 'charming, old–world courtesy,' as unfathomable as we could wish a magician to be.[57]

The most tantalising mystery of all surrounds the fate of his films. Some observers understood from the beginning their archival importance, arguing 'local films form a pictorial calendar of our city life of which there ought to be permanent record.[58] Sadly, film was and remained a commodity, not a resource – so many fourpences-a-foot. A film screened was a film consumed, and about as marketable

Figure 8. Walter Jeffs talking to Anna Neagle in Birmingham, 1937. *V. Price.*

as any other used goods. One drastic option was to cut them into short strips, each of a few frames, to sell as keepsakes; at the end of a Jeffs' run at Bristol in 1908 'specimens of film as used in the projection of the New Century Pictures' were offered in penny envelopes.[59] Judging by his fondness for quoting from that songbook to passing pleasures, Fitzgerald's *Omar Khayyam* ('Tis nothing but a magic shadow show, round which we phantom figures come and go') it was the fleetingness of film he cherished, not its staying power.[60]

A little hope is, however, permissible. We know that Jeffs retained certain subjects well beyond their immediate screen life: *Buffalo Bill's Parade* was revived in 1908, five years on, while in 1935 his *Birmingham military veterans at Cannon Hill Park*, dating from 1908, was shown at the Scala in Smallbrook Street;[61] there are unconfirmed later sightings, too. And in 1956 a box containing a thousand of Jeffs' glass lantern slides came to light in a Birmingham secondhand shop, priced at £1.[62] Legend has it his films somehow ended up in America. Precedent insists they are in your attic. Wherever, given the hundred–year lifespan of cellulose nitrate, they will soon have faded beyond recall, like dreams the morning after.[63]

Notes and References

1. *Bioscope*, 2.11.11.
2. Iris Barry, *Let's go to the pictures*, London: Chatto & Windus, 1926, p240.
3. Quoted in Bird John, *Cinema Parade*, Birmingham: Cornish 1947, p IX, written by a friend of Jeff's, this book is the best source on his life and work.
4. *Sunday Mercury*, 28.2.60.
5. Seasons varied from a few weeks (1902) to nine months (1911).
6. Advert, *The Owl*, 6.9.07. For New Century Pictures, see Mellor G J, *Picture Palaces*, Newcastle

on Tyne: Frank Graham, 1971, p23; *Birmingham Programme of Amusements*, 27.8.06; advert, *Midland Amusements*, 23.12.11; Bioscope, 4.1.17.

7. Midland Amusements, 7.3.10.

8. For one of these remarkable occasions, see *Birmingham Post*, 13.11.09.

9. For Hamilton's Excursions, see Matthison A L L, *In reply to yours*, Birmingham: Cornish, 1945, pp 119–121; *Birmingham Weekly Post*, 3.12.54.

10. Note the hyphen. For Thomas A D, see Barnes John, Pioneers of British film, London: Bishopsgate Press, 1983, pp 77–9; Bird J, *ibid.*, pp 45–6.

11. Advert, *Birmingham Daily Gazette*, 6.5.01.

12. The *Owl*, 31.5.01.

13. Advert, *Birmingham Daily Gazette*, 4.5.01.

14. The *Owl*, 10.5.01.

15. *Birmingham Daily Gazette*, 7.5.01.

16. The *Owl*, 4.10.01.

17. *Birmingham Daily Gazette*, 4.6.01.

18. Advert, the *Owl*, 17.5.01.

19. Advert, *Birmingham Daily Gazette*, 29.6.01.

20. The *Era*, 9.10.1897.

21. *Birmingham Daily Mail*, 7.7.22.

22. The *Owl*, 31.5.01.

23. *Birmingham Daily Mail*, 9.7.01.

24. The *Owl*, 26.6.03.

25. See the *Owl*, 31.5.01; *Birmingham Evening Despatch*, 5.10.06; *Birmingham Daily Post*, 17.9.10.

26. The *Owl*, 17.7.09.

27. Bird J, *ibid.*, p 75.

28. Advert, the *Owl*, 10.5.01.

29. *Birmingham Daily Mail*, 3.9.02.

30. *Birmingham Evening Despatch*, 9.7.06.

31. *Birmingham Daily Gazette*, 9.6.03.

32. The *Owl*, 12.6.03.

33. See Bird, J, *ibid*, pp 11, 30; *Birmingham Post*, 16.9.52.

34. For Jeffs' sole fiction film, *A father's vengeance*, shot at Coleshill, see Bird, J, *ibid.*, pp 26–7.

35. Barry, Iris, *ibid*, pp 240–1.

36. Advert, the *Owl*, 6.9.07.

37. See the photograph in the *Birmingham Mail*, 14.4.56.

38. *Birmingham Programme of Amusements*, 6.8.06.

39. *Birmingham Daily Gazette*, 19.9.11.

40. Advert, *Birmingham Programme of Amusements*, 15.1.06.

41. *Midland Amusements*, 28.10.11.

42. *Birmingham Daily Gazette*, 7.5.01.

43. The *Owl*, 18.10.01.

44. Balcon, Michael, *Michael Balcon presents a lifetime of films*, London: Hutchinson, 1969, p8.

45. For Engleman Joseph, see Josephs Zoe (ed), *Birmingham Jewry: more aspects, 1740–1930*, Birmingham: Birmingham Jewish History Research Group, 1984, pp 117–9; *Birmingham Programme of Amusements*, 3.9.06; *Birmingham Mail*, 24.9.43.

46. Bird, J, *ibid*, p 30.

47. *Ibid*, p 24.

48. Musser, Charles, *The emergence of cinema*, Berkeley: University of California Press, 1994, p223.

49. The *Owl*, 22.11.07.

50. Advert, the *Owl*, 15.11.07.

51. Advert, *Birmingham Weekly Mercury*, 11.12.09.

52. *The Picture House, New Street, Opening Brochure*, 20.10.10.

53. see *Published Minutes, City of Birmingham Annual Licensing Meetings*, 8.2.12.

54. *Bioscope*, 11.4.12.

55. See Stratford–on–Avon Public Records Office, Deposit DR 594, *Papers of Waller Jeffs.*

56. Winfield Sam, *Dream palaces of Derby*, Derby: Winfield, 1995, p 8. See also Mellor, *ibid*, pp 34–5.

57. Bird, J, *ibid*, p 19; *Stratford-on-Avon Herald*, 4.7.41.

58. The *Owl*, 14.8.03.

59. *Bioscope*, 17.12.08.

60. Advert, the *Owl*, 6.9.07.

61. See *Birmingham Evening Despatch*, 7.3.35.

62. See *Birmingham Gazette*, 26.4.56.

63. Thanks are due to Richard Albutt, Joseph McKenna and Dudley

THE EDITOR

Brian Hall is a Senior Lecturer in the School of Information Studies at the University of Central England in Birmingham. He has been teaching a module on the information resources for local studies for thirty years and has trained many of this country's local studies librarians, particularly in Birmingham and the Black Country. He has supervised hundreds of local history projects and dissertations by his students at BA, MA and PhD levels. His own work in local history has revolved mainly around population studies, canals, family history and the history of libraries, and included a number of projects undertaken for his Master's degree at Loughborough University.

He was a founder member of the Library Association's Local Studies Group and was its first national secretary for nine years.

He is currently the Hon. Secretary of the West Midland Branch of the Library Association. In his 'spare time' (sic) he is an enthusiastic cricket umpire in the Birmingham & District League.

ACKNOWLEDGEMENTS

My grateful thanks are due to all the contributors for being so positive to my invitations to produce chapters for this book. In particular, thanks are due to Patrick Baird and his team in the History and Local Studies Department of Birmingham Reference Library for coping with my impossible demands at such notice. I should also like to place on record my gratitude to Judith Vernon for her invaluable editorial and indexing advice.

ILLUSTRATIONS

Many of the illustrations in this book are reproduced from originals in Birmingham Reference Library and thanks must go to the staff for their help in locating them. I also need to thank Ann Firth, Roger Ward, Chris Brockie and Val Hart for supplying some of their own materials for reproduction. A special note of thanks needs to be accorded to Victor Price for his permission to reproduce some of the materials used in the chapter on Waller Jeffs.

While every effort has been made to establish ownership of the copyright of the illustrations used in this book, it is possible that some may have slipped through the net. Copyright holders are asked to contact the editor in such cases.

CONTRIBUTORS

1. BIRMINGHAM WORKHOUSE MASTERS AND MATRONS IN THE 1830S AND 1840S

Paul Tolley was born in Birmingham and lived in King's Heath before moving to his current home in the north of the city. He gained a BA in librarianship from the City of Birmingham Polytechnic in 1983 and has since worked in both libraries and bookselling.

Since 1995 he has worked at the University of Central England Library as a cataloguer.

Like his parents he has always had a keen interest in history, including local history, and having gained his BA decided to embark on a part-time MA in Modern History and Political Studies at Coventry Polytechnic, which he obtained in 1987. Subsequently, he studies part-time for a PhD on the Poor Law history of Birmingham at De Montfort University, Leicester, which he gained in 1995.

2. SOME LESSER KNOWN CHARACTERS OF BIRMINGHAM

Patrick Baird is Joint Head of Local Studies and History Service, Birmingham Central Library.

He was born in Moseley, Birmingham and educated at St Philip's Grammar School, Edgbaston. He has been employed by the library service since leaving school, including a period as a junior assistant at Kings Norton library.

After gaining his professional qualification at the School of Librarianship, Birmingham College of Commerce, now University of Central England, he was appointed as Schools Liaison Librarian in 1973 and Head of the Local Studies service in 1981.

He has been involved in a number of activities connected with local history including the foundation of The Birmingham and District Local History Association and he is President of two Birmingham local history societies.

He represents the Birmingham Civic Society on the Sir Barry Jackson Trust at the Repertory Theatre and is a member of the Birmingham Breakfast Rotary Club.

He is the author of *A Century of Birmingham - Events of Events, People and Places over the Last 100 Years*, published in 2000.

3. THE PAGEANT OF BIRMINGHAM

Richard Albutt was born in Birmingham in 1954 and attended Kings Norton Boys Grammar School. He studied librarianship at Birmingham Polytechnic (now UCE) and has worked in libraries since 1975.

For the last twelve years he has been part of Birmingham Central libraries Local Studies and History Service working as Education Liaison Librarian and currently as Community History Development Librarian. He is responsible for the promotion of local history resources in the Central and Community Libraries, together with the initiating of projects, which lead to the further development of these collections. For the past eight years he has been responsible for the Library's History Van project, which takes resources out into the community and encourages the donation of digital images by local communities.

4. BIRMINGHAM AND THE SPANISH CIVIL WAR

Peter Drake is one of the two service heads in the Local Studies section of Birmingham Central Library. He has spent most of his librarianship career in different departments in the Reference Library.

He was awarded a MLitt from Birmingham University for a thesis on The Labour Party and the Spanish Civil War. Subsequently he has contributed entries on Birmingham labour leaders to the Dictionary of Labour Biography, written articles about Birmingham during the General Strike and for the Birmingham labour newspaper *The Town Crier*.

More recently he has compiled a number of photographic histories of Birmingham suburbs and has just completed a history of Bangladeshis in Birmingham.

5. THE CHILDREN'S EMIGRATION HOMES

Val Hart started out as a history graduate and trained as an archivist before working as a teacher and community worker at St. Paul's Community Project.

She has lived in Birmingham for the last thirty years and has published a book on the history of Balsall Heath.

Val is a founder member of the 'Making History' reminiscence theatre group and enjoys working creatively on local history topics with all ages in a community setting.

6. FIT AND PROPER COUNCILLORS?

Margaret Holmes is a Londoner by birth but has lived in Birmingham for the last nine years. She has three grown-up children, Tom, Rosie and Luke. With more free time on her hands she was able to study for an Honours Degree in Government at the University of Central England in Birmingham. Her particular interests on the course were Birmingham history and local government, hence her dissertation on Birmingham City Council which forms the basis for this contribution to *Aspects of Birmingham*. Following her degree she represented Bournville as a Labour Councillor on the City Council for four years – 'a very interesting and educational experience'. Whilst doing this she worked part-time as a social research interviewer, a job which she still does.

During the last two years she has become a practising Buddhist and has become increasingly fascinated by this discipline, and involved at the local centre in Birmingham. Also, she has practised yoga for many years and hopes to train as a yoga teacher in the near future. She continues to enjoy writing although this is her is her first publication – not counting letters to newspapers!

7. BIRMINGHAM MUNICIPAL BANK

Chris Brockie is a local government officer who has worked for various parish and metropolitan councils. He is currently Senior Community Economic Development Officer at Birmingham City Council. His responsibilities include the strategic development of credit unions and community enterprises. Chris' research interests include financial exclusion. His undergraduate dissertation was on the history of the Birmingham Municipal Bank and his Master's thesis was on public policy towards credit union development in Britain. He is now investigating the nature of social capital for his doctorate.

8. THE BIRMINGHAM MISSION

Ann Firth's interest in local history goes back to her childhood days when, even then, she wanted to know more about a person, a place, or a building – why it was built, who lived in it or even why it was where it was. It was not until she took early retirement in 1997 that her interest finally took a practical step.

A free course 'The Industrial Revolution' was on offer on Saturday mornings at Matthew Boulton College. The course was led by Toby McLeod who afterwards offered the class another course on the Victorian Era.

She now does her own researches including items for the West Midland Research Group of which she is a member.

9. MONUMENTAL SOLDIER

After studying at the Universities of London and Cambridge, **Roger Ward** became a schoolmaster in London. In 1963 he was appointed to teach history at the City of Birmingham College of Education. There he developed his interest in local history and developed courses on the history of Birmingham. In 1973 he moved as a Senior Lecturer to Birmingham Polytechnic, later the University of Central England, where he spent the rest of his career, retiring as a Principal Lecturer in 1997. His course on the history of Birmingham became a popular fixture on the BA Politics course, especially for part-time students working in local government. He has also lectured very widely to local groups and organisations and has published articles on such key figures as Joseph Chamberlain and John Bright.

He is an Honorary Research Fellow of the Department of Public Policy and is currently engaged in writing a political history of Birmingham.

10. HAZELWOOD AND THE HILLS

Dr Chris Upton is a Senior Lecturer in history at Newman College of Higher Education in Birmingham.

He is the author of *History of Birmingham*, *History of Wolverhampton* and his latest work, *History of Lichfield*. He has also contributed to local history writings through his weekly columns and feature articles in the *Birmingham Post*. He is Editor of the *Birmingham Historian* and was history adviser to the 'Think-Tank', the Birmingham Museum of Science and Discovery at the newly opened Millennium Point. Chris has an MA from Cambridge and obtained his PhD at St Andrew's University. Before taking up his present post he was a community liaison librarian in the History and Local Studies department of Birmingham Reference Library.

11. INTRODUCING WALLER JEFFS

Christopher Dingley writes and researches local film history and makes occasional short films at neglected places in the city centre.

He is currently writing a 'Who was Who' of Birmingham people who contributed to cinema's first century.

GENERAL INDEX

Indexes compiled by Judith Vernon

NAME INDEX